CW01302767

Discovering Orthodox Christianity

A Beginner's Guide to the Orthodox Christian Church

Authored & Compiled by
Alexander Egger
Contributions by
Fr. Antony Balnaves

Independently Published
by Nevsky Publications
- 2025 -

Nevsky Publications
Published by Nevsky Publications
Independent Researcher
www.nevskypublications.com
ISBN: 9798308717898
Copyright © 2025

All rights reserved under international copyright conventions. No part of the text in this book may be reproduced or utilized in any manner in any form or by any means whatsoever, including electronic or mechanical, including photocopying, scanning, recording, or by any information storage and retrieval system, without written permission except in the case of brief quotations embodied in critical articles and reviews.

The text in this book is sold subject to the condition that it shall not, by way of trade or otherwise, be lent, re-sold, hired out, or otherwise circulated without the publisher's prior consent in any form of binding or cover other than in which it is published and without a similar condition including this condition imposed on the subsequent purchaser.

Scripture taken from the St. Athanasius Academy Septuagint™. Copyright © 2008 by St. Athanasius Academy of Orthodox Theology. Used by permission. All rights reserved.

Scripture taken from the New King James Version®. Copyright © 1982 by Thomas Nelson. Used by permission. All rights reserved.

"Every Christian should find for himself the imperative and incentive to become holy. If you live without struggle and without hope of becoming holy, then you are Christians only in name and not in essence. But without holiness, no one shall see the Lord, that is to say they will not attain eternal blessedness. It is a trustworthy saying that Jesus Christ came into the world to save sinners (I Tim. 1:15). But we deceive ourselves if we think that we are saved while remaining sinners. Christ saves those sinners by giving them the means to become saints."

- St. Philaret of Moscow,

Sermon of September 23, 1847

Contents

The Lord's Prayer 9

What is Orthodoxy? 10
   Orthodoxy: Faith and Action as One 10
   Worship in Spirit and Truth 11
   The Importance of Prayer and Asceticism 11
   The Sacraments: Pathways to Divine Grace 12
   Theosis: Becoming Partakers of the Divine Nature 13
   Balance in the Orthodox Life 13
   Orthodoxy's Call to Spiritual Union with God 14

What Do Orthodox Christians Believe? 15
   Apostolic Succession and Unity 15
   The Teachings of the Church 16
   Orthodox Belief and the Meaning of "Orthodox" 16
   Theosis: The Aim of Christian Life 17
   Monasticism and Its Role in Orthodox Spirituality 17
   The Role of Saints and Martyrs 18
   The Sacraments: The Means of Grace 18
   Ecumenism and Orthodox Unity 18

Orthodox Teachings and Key Terms 21
   God the Father 21
   Jesus Christ 21
   Incarnation 21
   The Holy Spirit 22
   Sin 22

Salvation	22
Baptism	23
New Birth	23
Justification	24
Sanctification	24
The Bible	24
Worship	25
Communion (Eucharist)	25
Communion of Saints	25
Confession	26
Discipline in the Church	26
The Holy Theotokos	27
Prayer to the Saints	27
Apostolic Succession	28
Church Councils	29
Creed	30
Spiritual Gifts	30
The Second Coming	31
Heaven	31
Hell	32
Creation	32
Things to Know for a First Visit to an Orthodox Church	**33**
The Church Building	33
Stand Up, Stand Up for Jesus	43
Sign of the Cross	44
Clergy Etiquette	47
Kneeling, Prostrating?	50

Act of Kissing	51
Blessed Bread and Consecrated Bread	53
Where's the General Confession?	56
The Role of the Priest's Wife	57
Singing and Chanting	58
The Timeless Rhythm of Orthodox Liturgy	60
The Divine Liturgy	62
The Three Doors	68
Holy Relics: A Testament to the Sanctity of the Saints	70
The Candle: A Light of Faith and Devotion	75
Behavior in Church	77
Punctuality and Respect in Church	79
Fasting Before the Divine Liturgy	79
The Necessity of Regular Attendance	80
Entering the Church and Acts of Reverence	80
Conduct During Services	81
Men and Women's Placement in the Church	82
The Sacred Atmosphere of the Church	82
Kissing Icons and Prostrations	82
Full Prostrations and Their Significance	83
The Sacredness of Communal Prayer	86
Guidelines for Proper Church Etiquette	87
The Importance of Sacred Space	89
On Venerating the Holy Gospels, the Cross, Holy Relics, and Icons	90
Prayers When Venerating Icons and the Cross	91
Sanctified Bread in the Orthodox Tradition	92

The Prosphoron: Offering Bread 93
The Artos: Symbol of the Risen Christ 94
Antidoron: Bread for the Faithful 95
Sanctified Bread During Vigil 95
Church Commemoration Lists: Guidelines and Importance .96
Timing of Submission 96
Writing with a Prayerful Heart 96
Order and Format of Names 97
Specific Considerations 98
Offering Commemoration Lists 98

A Christian Home 100
The Christian Home: Simplicity and Spirituality 101
The Family Church: A Place of Worship and Salvation 102
The Blessing of the Home and Family as a Church 103
Spiritual Protection and the Power of Holy Objects 104
The Christian Home as a Place of Forgiveness 105
Fasting and Asceticism in the Christian Home 106
The Family Church as the Path to Salvation 106
Home Prayer Corner or Room 107
A Journey into the Heart of Orthodox Worship 114

Concluding Statement on Christianity and Orthodoxy 116
The Defense Against Heresy: The Battle for Orthodoxy 117
The Triumph of Orthodoxy 119
The Preservation of Orthodox Doctrine: A Call to Vigilance 120
Orthodoxy as the True Faith 120

References & Sources 123

THE LORD'S PRAYER

Our Father who art in heaven, hallowed be Thy name, Thy kingdom come, Thy will be done on earth as it is in heaven. Give us this day our daily bread, and forgive us our trespasses as we forgive those who trespass against us, and lead us not into temptation, but deliver us from evil. Amen.

(Matthew 6:9-13 and Luke 11:2-4).

☦

Отче наш, Иже еси на небесе́х! Да святится имя Твое, да прии́дет Царствие Твое, да будет воля Твоя, яко на небеси́ и на земли́. Хлеб наш насущный да́ждь нам дне́сь; и оста́ви нам до́лги наша, якоже и мы оставляем должнико́м нашим; и не введи нас во искушение, но изба́ви нас от лукаваго. Яко Твое есть Царство и сила, и слава, Отца, и Сына, и Святаго Духа, ныне и присно, и во веки веков. Аминь.

(Мф.6:9-13 и Лк.11:2-4).

WHAT IS ORTHODOXY?

As Archpriest Victor Potapov said, Orthodoxy, at its core, is the true faith in God. It represents the unwavering strength that guides each faithful Orthodox Christian along the righteous and pious path. To be Orthodox means not only to believe but to align the mind, heart, and voice with the truth that God has revealed about Himself, creation, humanity, and the purpose of life. This faith leads us toward spiritual union with Him and the promise of eternal salvation. As the Apostle Paul teaches, "Without faith, it is impossible to please God" (Hebrews 11:6), but Orthodoxy reminds us that this faith must be lived, acted upon, and embodied in every aspect of life.

Orthodoxy: Faith and Action as One

Orthodoxy is more than simply adhering to the right beliefs and confessing the fundamental truths and dogmas of the Church of Christ. It is a living faith, one that calls believers to actively embody the teachings of Christ through virtuous living and unwavering fulfillment of God's commandments. The faith of the Orthodox Christian cannot exist in isolation from works; it is realized through humility, meekness, love for one's neighbor, and serving the Church and those in need. As the Apostle James reminds us, "Faith without works is dead" (James 2:26), and the Lord Himself promises to "reward every man according to his works" (Matthew 16:27). This principle is reiterated by the Apostle Paul, who writes, "Every man shall receive his own reward according to his own labor" (1 Corinthians 3:8).

In Orthodoxy, faith and works are inseparable, like soul and body, guiding the faithful towards a deeper communion with God. This union of faith and works reflects the Church's teaching that salvation is a synergy between God's grace and human effort. While salvation is a gift from God, freely offered, human beings must respond to this gift with a life of virtue, prayer, and love for others.

Worship in Spirit and Truth

Orthodoxy also embodies the correct and proper worship of God. Christ taught that, "God is Spirit, and those who worship Him must worship in spirit and truth" (John 4:24). The divine services of the Orthodox Church, deeply rooted in Scripture and Sacred Tradition, are filled with prayer, reverence, and symbolic acts that elevate the human soul toward God. These services are not merely formal rituals but are sacred acts of worship that engage the whole person—body, soul, and mind—in offering glory to God. The Church's liturgical life reflects the mystery and beauty of the heavenly kingdom, a foretaste of which is experienced during the Divine Liturgy.

The Importance of Prayer and Asceticism

In Orthodoxy, prayer is not only an obligation but the lifeblood of the Christian journey. As St. Paul exhorts, "Pray without ceasing" (1 Thessalonians 5:17), the Orthodox Christian is called to make prayer a constant presence in their life, whether through communal worship or personal devotion. The Jesus Prayer, "***Lord Jesus Christ, Son of God, have mercy on me, a sinner***," is one of the most beloved and profound prayers in the Orthodox tradition. It encapsulates the essence of repentance, humility, and the constant remembrance of God's mercy.

Alongside prayer, asceticism plays a critical role in Orthodox spirituality. The Church calls its faithful to engage in practices such as fasting, vigilance, and abstinence, not as ends in themselves, but as means of drawing closer to God. Fasting, for example, teaches self-discipline and reminds the faithful that spiritual nourishment is more important than physical sustenance, as Christ said, "Man shall not live by bread alone" (Matthew 4:4). These ascetic practices help to balance the intellect, heart, will, and body, ensuring that each aspect of life is oriented towards God.

The Sacraments: Pathways to Divine Grace

Integral to the life of every Orthodox Christian is participation in the Holy Mysteries (Sacraments). These sacred rites are considered channels of divine grace, through which believers are united more closely with Christ and His Church. The Eucharist, in particular, is the source and summit of Christian life. In receiving the Body and Blood of Christ, the faithful are mystically united with Him and with one another. As St. Irenaeus of Lyons taught, "Our Faith is in accord with the Eucharist, and the Eucharist confirms our Faith." The Eucharist is not merely symbolic, but it is Christ HIMSELF in His True Body and Blood among His people, a mystery that transcends human understanding.

Other sacraments, such as Baptism, Chrismation, Confession, Matrimony, and Unction, play essential roles in sanctifying various aspects of life and bringing the faithful into deeper communion with God. Each sacrament is a tangible manifestation of God's grace at work in the life of the Church, transforming the faithful and strengthening them for the Christian journey.

Theosis: Becoming Partakers of the Divine Nature

One of the most profound teachings of Orthodoxy is the concept of *theosis*, or deification. Theosis refers to the process by which human beings, through grace, become partakers of the divine nature (2 Peter 1:4). This does not mean that humans become gods by nature, but rather, by grace, they are transformed into the likeness of God. Theosis is the goal of Christian life, achieved through participation in the sacraments, prayer, and the cultivation of virtues. It is the fulfillment of Christ's promise of eternal life, in which the faithful are united with God, sharing in His life and love.

Balance in the Orthodox Life

Orthodoxy places a strong emphasis on balance in the Christian life. This balance encompasses intellect, heart, will, labor, prayer, abstinence, and vigilance. Each of these elements must have its rightful place in the life of a believer. Orthodoxy teaches that only through this harmony can we truly grow closer to God. The ascetic practices of the Church, such as fasting and vigil, are balanced with the joyful participation in the sacraments and communal worship. This balance is reflected in the Church's liturgical calendar, which alternates between periods of fasting and feasting, reminding the faithful of the need for both repentance and celebration in their spiritual lives.

Orthodoxy's Call to Spiritual Union with God

Orthodoxy, at its heart, is the path to spiritual union with God. It is not only about right belief but about living a life that reflects the teachings of Christ through humility, love, and service. This life, centered on prayer, the sacraments, and a deep commitment to God's commandments, leads the faithful toward the ultimate goal of salvation—union with God in Christ.

In today's world, where many competing ideologies and religious movements claim to possess the truth, Orthodoxy stands firm as the unchanging witness to the fullness of faith. Through its preservation of the Apostolic tradition,[1] the teachings of the Holy Fathers, and its unwavering commitment to Christ, Orthodoxy continues to guide the faithful on the path to eternal life.

In this book, we will refrain from comparing Orthodoxy to other so-called denominations or engaging in criticisms or polemics against heterodox beliefs. Orthodoxy that defines itself primarily through opposition to other faith traditions risks becoming a shallow or "weak" Orthodoxy, one that overlooks its own profound depth, richness, and truth. Instead, we will focus on presenting the essence and beauty of Orthodox Christianity on its own terms. The task of making detailed comparisons or critiques is best left to those with greater wisdom and a clearer grasp of historical context. Here, our aim is to offer an authentic portrayal of Orthodox belief and practice, allowing its distinctiveness to speak for itself.

---

[1] **Apostolic Tradition**: The teachings, practices, and authority passed down from the Apostles to their successors through both written Scripture and oral teachings. It forms the foundation of the Church's doctrine, worship, and governance, ensuring the continuity and unity of the Christian faith.

WHAT DO ORTHODOX CHRISTIANS BELIEVE?

Almost two thousand years ago, Jesus Christ, the Son of God, came into the world to establish His Church through His Apostles and disciples, providing a path to salvation for all of humanity. In the years that followed, His Apostles spread the Good News far and wide, founding churches throughout the known world. These churches were united in one faith, one worship, and in partaking of the Holy Mysteries (known in the West as the Sacraments) of the Church.

Among the most ancient of these are the Patriarchates of Constantinople, Alexandria, Antioch, Jerusalem, and Rome, all directly founded by the Apostles. St. Andrew founded the Church of Constantinople, St. Mark established the Church in Alexandria, St. Paul initiated the Church in Antioch, and Sts. Peter and James built the Church of Jerusalem. Sts. Peter and Paul together established the Church of Rome. Through missionary work in later centuries, the Orthodox Church expanded further, founding additional churches, such as those in Russia, Greece, Serbia, Bulgaria, and Romania.

Apostolic Succession and Unity

Each of the above churches is independent in administration, yet all—except the Church of Rome, which separated in 1054—remain united in faith, doctrine, Apostolic tradition, and worship. This unity is maintained through Apostolic Succession, an unbroken line of bishops that traces directly back to the Apostles. The bishops, as the successors to the Apostles, serve as the guardians of both Holy Scripture and Sacred Tradition, ensuring that the faith and teachings of Christ remain unbroken. Through the continuous preservation of Apostolic Succession, the Orthodox Church safeguards the truth of the Gospel as it was given by Christ and passed down through the generations.

The Teachings of the Church

The teachings of the Orthodox Church rest on two primary pillars: Holy Scripture and Sacred Tradition. Sacred Tradition not only predates the written Scriptures but also provides the context and interpretation necessary to fully understand them. As the Gospel of St. John attests, "There are also many other things which Jesus did, the which, if they should be written every one, I suppose that even the world itself could not contain the books that should be written" (John 21:25). Much of what was transmitted orally by the Apostles has been preserved within this living Tradition of the Church. These teachings were safeguarded through the Seven Ecumenical Councils, which addressed critical doctrinal matters, including the nature of Christ, the Holy Trinity, and the rejection of heresies. These councils solidified the Orthodox Church's theology and ensured that all local churches remained unified in doctrine and worship.

Orthodox Belief and the Meaning of "Orthodox"

The word "Orthodox" itself means "right teaching" or "right worship," derived from the Greek words *orthos* (right) and *doxa* (teaching or worship). As divisions and false teachings arose in the early Christian era, the term "Orthodox" became the identifier for the Church that faithfully preserved the true teachings of Christ. The Orthodox Church remains vigilant in guarding the truth against error and schism, both for the protection of its faithful and to glorify Christ, who is the head of the Church.

In today's religious landscape, countless groups claim to be successors of the early Christian Church, often teaching very different doctrines. To navigate this, a yardstick of truth is essential—one that compares contemporary teachings with what the Church has always believed, from the time of the Apostles. While everyone has the freedom and will to choose what to believe, it is wise to explore and understand the authentic faith that Christ entrusted to His Church.

Theosis: The Aim of Christian Life

At the heart of Orthodox Christianity is the concept of *theosis*, or deification, which is the goal of human life. Through participation in the sacraments, prayer, and the cultivation of virtues, believers are called to become partakers of the divine nature (2 Peter 1:4). This process of growing closer to God, becoming more like Him in holiness and love, is the central aim of Orthodox Christian life. *Theosis* is not achieved by human effort alone but through the grace of God, made accessible through the life of the Church.

Monasticism and Its Role in Orthodox Spirituality

Monasticism plays a significant role in the Orthodox Church, serving as a model of asceticism and spiritual discipline. Monastics dedicate their lives to prayer, fasting, and humility, often becoming spiritual guides for the faithful. The monastic tradition, particularly on Mount Athos and other monastic centers, preserves the highest ideals of Christian life. Through their prayers, monastics contribute to the spiritual well-being of the Church as a whole, embodying the call to *theosis* in a life of radical devotion to God.

The Role of Saints and Martyrs

The Orthodox Church venerates saints and martyrs as exemplars of Christian holiness and steadfastness in the faith. Saints are those who have fully embodied the life of Christ, whether through martyrdom, asceticism, or charitable works. Their relics are venerated as tangible connections to God's grace, and their intercessions are sought by the faithful in times of need. Martyrs, who gave their lives for Christ, hold a special place of honor in the Church, reminding believers of the ultimate witness of faith.

The Sacraments: The Means of Grace

The Orthodox Church's sacramental life is central to its theology and spirituality. In addition to the Eucharist, which is the pinnacle of Christian worship, the Church celebrates seven Holy Mysteries (Sacraments): Baptism, Chrismation, Confession, the Eucharist, Holy Matrimony, Ordination, and Unction. These sacraments are not mere symbols but are understood as real means by which the faithful receive the grace of the Holy Spirit. Each sacrament offers a unique encounter with God's presence and strengthens the believer's journey toward *theosis*.

Ecumenism and Orthodox Unity

The Orthodox Church recognizes the desire for Christian unity, but it insists that true unity can only be achieved by rediscovering and returning to the fullness of Orthodoxy. The Russian Orthodox Church Abroad has always maintained a cautious and strictly

Orthodox stance toward ecumenism,[2] grounded in the teachings of the Holy Fathers. In a statement from December 31, 1931, the Russian Church Abroad reaffirmed its commitment to preserving the Faith of the One, Holy, Catholic, and Apostolic Church, while recognizing the separation of those who have fallen away.

The Ecumenical Movement, however, is largely shaped by a Protestant view of the Church, which suggests that no single Christian denomination possesses the entire truth. Instead, they believe each group holds fragments of truth that can be united through dialogue and joint worship. From an Orthodox perspective, this approach is fundamentally flawed. The Orthodox Church professes that it alone has preserved the fullness of Truth, given on the day of Pentecost, and therefore, there is no need to piece together scattered truths.

For Orthodox Christians, joint prayer and Communion at the Liturgy are expressions of an already existing unity within the One, Holy, Catholic, and Apostolic Church. As St. Irenaeus of Lyons[3] stated in the 2nd century: "Our Faith is in accord with the Eucharist, and the Eucharist confirms our Faith." The Holy

---

[2] **Ecumenism**: The movement or efforts aimed at promoting unity and cooperation among Christian denominations and, in a broader sense, among all religions. Rooted in the desire for reconciliation and understanding, ecumenism seeks to overcome divisions within Christianity and foster dialogue, mutual respect, and shared witness to the faith while maintaining doctrinal integrity.

[3] **St. Irenaeus of Lyons**: A 2nd-century bishop, theologian, and Church Father (ca. 130–202), renowned for his defense of orthodox Christianity against heresies, particularly Gnosticism. As the Bishop of Lyons, he authored Against Heresies (Adversus Haereses), a seminal work emphasizing the unity of Scripture, Apostolic Tradition, and the Incarnation of Christ. St. Irenaeus is celebrated for his role in shaping early Christian theology and his assertion that the Church's teaching authority is rooted in the Apostolic succession. His feast day is commemorated on June 28th / July 11th.

Fathers teach that the Church is the Body of Christ, and its members participate in this Body through the Eucharist. Without the Eucharist, there is no Church. Therefore, intercommunion with those outside the Orthodox Church would falsely suggest a unity that does not yet exist, obscuring the deep dogmatic and ecclesiastical divisions that still plague the Christian world.

ORTHODOX TEACHINGS AND KEY TERMS

God the Father

God the Father is the source and fountainhead of the Holy Trinity. In the Holy Scriptures, God is revealed as Three Persons—Father, Son, and Holy Spirit—each sharing the same divine essence. From the Father, the Son is eternally begotten (Psalm 2:7, 2 Corinthians 11:31), and the Holy Spirit eternally proceeds (John 15:26). All creation came into being through the Son, in the Holy Spirit (Genesis 1–2; John 1:3). God the Father loves humanity so profoundly that He sent His only Son for the salvation of the world (John 3:16).

Jesus Christ

Jesus Christ, the Second Person of the Holy Trinity, is eternally begotten of the Father. He is both fully God and fully man, having taken on human flesh through the Virgin Mary. The Nicene Creed, recited in every Orthodox Liturgy, proclaims Jesus as the only-begotten Son of God, consubstantial with the Father. His Incarnation, Crucifixion, and Resurrection are central to Christian salvation, fulfilling the Old Testament prophecies and ensuring eternal life for those who believe in Him.

Incarnation

The Incarnation is the mystery of Jesus Christ assuming human nature while remaining fully divine. Through His birth from the Virgin Mary, Jesus becomes both God and man, embracing the limitations of human flesh to redeem humanity. This is a core truth of Christianity, for without the Incarnation, there is no salvation. St. John teaches, "Every spirit that does not confess that Jesus Christ has come in the flesh is not of God" (1 John 4:3). Through His Incarnation, Christ restores human nature and invites us to partake in His glorified humanity.

The Holy Spirit

The Holy Spirit is the third Person of the Holy Trinity, one in essence with the Father and the Son. Orthodox Christians confess the Holy Spirit as the Giver of Life, Who proceeds from the Father and is worshipped alongside the Father and the Son. The Holy Spirit empowers the Church, bestows spiritual gifts (1 Corinthians 12:7-13), and works in the lives of believers, guiding them toward holiness. The Holy Spirit is received at Baptism through Chrismation, marking the beginning of a lifelong journey of spiritual growth.

Sin

Sin is defined as missing the mark of God's divine will. It is the distortion of the good gifts God has given, separating humanity from God (Isaiah 59:1-2). St. Paul affirms, "All have sinned and fall short of the glory of God" (Romans 3:23). In His mercy, God offers forgiveness when we confess our sins (1 John 1:9). Christ, through His humanity, overcomes sin and redeems us, allowing for the restoration of our relationship with God.

Salvation

Salvation is the divine process by which humanity is delivered from sin, death, and eternal separation from God. It begins with repentance, baptism, and the receiving of the Holy Spirit (Acts

2:38). Salvation is not just a momentary event but a lifelong journey of growing in union with Christ through faith and the power of the Holy Spirit. Orthodox theology teaches that we are being saved, continually transforming into the image of God through participation in the life of the Church and the sacraments.

Baptism

Baptism is the sacrament through which one is united to Christ, receiving the forgiveness of sins and new life in the Holy Spirit. The Apostle Paul describes baptism as a participation in the death and resurrection of Christ (Romans 6:1-6). Orthodox Christians practice baptism by full immersion, symbolizing the complete renewal of the person. Baptism is more than a symbolic act; it is a mystical union with Christ, marking the beginning of salvation.

New Birth

The New Birth is the reception of new life in Christ, granting entrance into God's kingdom and His Church. Jesus explained this profound mystery by saying, "Unless one is born of water and the Spirit, he cannot enter the kingdom of God" (John 3:5). From the earliest days, the Church has taught that this refers to the waters of Baptism and the gift of the Holy Spirit. In Baptism, we are mystically united with Christ in His death, burial, and resurrection (Acts 2:38; Romans 6:3-4), being reborn into a new life. Contrary to modern interpretations that separate "being born again" from Baptism, the early Church understood this spiritual rebirth as integrally connected to Baptism—a truth with deep biblical foundations.

Justification

Justification in the Orthodox understanding is not merely a legal pronouncement, but a transformative reality in which we are forgiven and made righteous through Christ. It is not a one-time, instantaneous event guaranteeing eternal security, but a dynamic, ongoing process. As we walk in faith, relying on the grace and power of God, we grow in righteousness. Justification is an active pursuit of holiness, where the Christian participates in God's work, becoming ever more conformed to His image through obedience and love.

Sanctification

Sanctification is the process by which a person is set apart for God, growing in holiness and becoming like Christ through the work of the Holy Spirit. All believers are called to be saints, and this involves cooperating with God's grace, striving to live in accordance with His commandments. By the power of the Holy Spirit, we participate in this divine work, growing in holiness and union with God, striving to reflect His divine image in our lives.

The Bible

The Bible, the divinely inspired Word of God, is central to the life of the Church. It is not merely a historical document, but part of God's ongoing revelation to humanity. The Old Testament records the history of salvation from Creation to the time of the Prophets, while the New Testament contains the life of Jesus Christ, the writings of the Apostles, and the doctrines of the early Church. The New Testament canon, finalized by the early Church Fathers, is the foundation for Christian teaching, worship, and life.

The Scriptures remain at the heart of Orthodox worship and personal devotion, providing the framework for understanding God's will and His plan for humanity.

Worship

Worship in Orthodoxy is the offering of praise, glory, and thanksgiving to the Holy Trinity—Father, Son, and Holy Spirit. It goes beyond private devotion or simple acts of piety. The focus is on the corporate worship of the Church, especially through the Divine Liturgy, where the faithful come together to glorify God and partake of His divine presence. Orthodox worship is transformative, as the faithful enter into communion with God and the heavenly hosts, experiencing a foretaste of the Kingdom of Heaven.

Communion (Eucharist)

The Eucharist, meaning "thanksgiving," is central to Orthodox Christian life. In this sacrament, Orthodox Christians partake of Christ's true Body and Blood, which nourishes both soul and body. As Jesus commanded, "Do this in remembrance of Me" (Luke 22:19), the Eucharist is more than symbolic; it is the real participation in the life of Christ, making it the spiritual food that sustains the faithful. Early Christians referred to the Eucharist as the "medicine of immortality," recognizing its divine grace and power.

Communion of Saints

The Communion of Saints is the belief that those who have died in Christ remain an active part of the Church. The Saints, who are alive in the presence of God, continue to pray for those on earth, and their intercession is sought by Orthodox Christians. In the Eucharist, the Church on earth joins in worship with the Saints and angels in heaven, forming one united body in Christ. This communion reflects the eternal life promised to all who are united with Christ, both in this life and the next.

Confession

Confession is the open acknowledgment of one's sins before God, often done in the presence of a priest. It is a means of repentance, seeking forgiveness and spiritual healing. In the Orthodox Church, confession is not merely a formality but a sacramental act that brings the penitent into direct contact with God's mercy. As St. James teaches, "Confess your trespasses to one another, and pray for one another, that you may be healed" (James 5:16). Confession offers the assurance of forgiveness and the grace to overcome sin, restoring the believer to spiritual health and communion with God.

Discipline in the Church

Discipline within the Orthodox Church plays a vital role in maintaining the purity, holiness, and spiritual health of the community. It is not an act of punishment but a compassionate means to encourage repentance and renewal for those who have strayed from the faith. One significant form of discipline is excommunication, which involves exclusion from the sacraments, particularly Holy Communion. This form of correction is rooted in the New Testament, where St. Paul excommunicated a man in Corinth for unrepentant sin (1 Corinthians 5:1-5). The Apostle John also warned the faithful against welcoming or associating with those who reject Christ's truth (2 John 9-10). Throughout its history, the Church has exercised discipline with care and humility, always aiming to bring sinners back into communion with Christ through repentance and spiritual healing.

The Holy Theotokos

In Orthodox Christianity, Mary is honored with the title "Theotokos," which means "God-bearer" or "Mother of God." This title emphasizes her pivotal role in the mystery of the Incarnation, as she bore the Son of God in her womb and gave Him His human nature. When Elizabeth, the mother of John the Baptist, greeted Mary, she proclaimed, "The Mother of my Lord" (Luke 1:43), acknowledging the divine nature of the child she carried. Mary herself foretold that "all generations shall call me blessed" (Luke 1:48), and Orthodox Christians fulfill this prophecy by honoring her as the model of purity, obedience, and holiness. Orthodox veneration of Mary is not worship but a profound respect for the one who uniquely participated in God's plan of salvation by giving birth to Christ.

Prayer to the Saints

In Orthodox practice, praying to the saints is an expression of the Church's understanding of life beyond death. Physical death does not sever the relationship between Christians on earth and those who have departed to be with the Lord. The saints, having passed into eternal life, continue to be active members of the Church and intercede for those still on earth. Orthodox Christians seek their prayers, just as they would ask living friends and family to pray for them. The Book of Revelation and other scriptures affirm the saints' prayers before God's throne (Revelation 8:3), and Orthodox

Christians believe that the saints pray on behalf of the whole Church and even the entire world.

Apostolic Succession

Apostolic Succession refers to the unbroken transmission of spiritual authority from the Apostles through their successors, the bishops, via ordination. This practice, rooted in the earliest foundations of the Church, ensures the continuity of the faith, sacraments, and teachings, maintaining their fidelity to the Apostolic tradition. From the first centuries of Christianity, the Church has carefully preserved and defended Apostolic Succession against heretical claims of authority disconnected from this sacred lineage. The early Church Fathers diligently documented the lines of succession to affirm this essential continuity. Apostolic Succession is critical to preserving the unity of the Church. It guarantees that the Church remains anchored in the Apostolic faith, ensuring the transmission of truth through generations. Today, many groups have rejected this doctrine, leading to the fragmentation of Christianity into various denominations with differing interpretations of the faith. The Orthodox Church, however, holds firmly to the belief that the Church exists wherever three fundamental elements are present: Apostolic Succession, preservation of the Church's traditions and canons, and leadership under a right-believing bishop in Apostolic Succession. These core aspects define the Church, while administrative structures such as Patriarchates and autocephalous bodies are secondary to the unity provided by adherence to Holy Tradition.

In contrast, within the Roman Catholic Church, Apostolic Succession is uniquely tied to the office of the Pope, viewed as

Christ's Vicar on earth. While modern theologians have occasionally sought to redefine or downplay the centrality of the Papacy, the dogma of papal supremacy remains foundational to Roman Catholicism. Thus, when traditionalist Catholics separate from Rome due to liturgical or doctrinal concerns, they effectively sever themselves from the very source of authority within their own Church, as defined by Roman Catholic teaching. Without the centrality of Holy Tradition as in Orthodoxy, Catholic traditionalists lack a firm basis for such schisms.

Orthodox traditionalists, on the other hand, are not only justified but required by the Holy Canons to separate from bishops or churches that deviate from Holy Tradition. According to the Orthodox understanding, any Church or bishop that teaches heresy risks placing itself outside of the true faith, and the faithful are obligated to separate from it to preserve the integrity of the faith. This fundamental difference underscores a key contrast between Roman Catholicism and Orthodoxy: where Catholicism places authority in the Roman See, Orthodoxy places it in the wholeness of ecclesiastical tradition—the very body of the Church.

In essence, the divide between Roman Catholic and Orthodox traditionalists highlights a broader theological distinction: the Roman Church's reliance on the central authority of the Papacy, versus Orthodoxy's deep commitment to the authority found in the entirety of Apostolic Tradition and the collective unity of the Church.

Church Councils

Church councils have been instrumental in resolving theological disputes and maintaining the integrity of the Christian faith. The first significant council in Church history was the Council of Jerusalem, recorded in Acts 15, where the Apostles addressed the issue of whether Gentile converts needed to observe Jewish law. This established a pattern for convening councils to address pressing issues within the Church. Over the centuries, numerous local and regional councils have been held, but the most authoritative are the seven Ecumenical Councils, which are recognized by the Orthodox Church. These councils defined essential doctrines, including the nature of Christ, the Trinity, and the veneration of icons, and they remain a guiding force in Orthodox theology and practice.

Creed

The term "creed" comes from the Latin word *credo*, meaning "I believe." Creeds are formal statements of Christian belief, and they have been used by the Church since the earliest days to articulate and defend core doctrines. One of the most significant creeds is the Nicene Creed, formulated during the first two Ecumenical Councils in the fourth century. This creed was written in response to heresies that sought to undermine the divinity of Christ and the Holy Trinity. Orthodox Christians recite the Nicene Creed during the Divine Liturgy as a personal and communal affirmation of their faith, safeguarding the truth of the Christian doctrine against distortion.

Spiritual Gifts

The New Testament speaks of a variety of spiritual gifts given by the Holy Spirit to build up the Church and serve its members. These include apostleship, prophecy, evangelism, teaching, healing, and more (1 Corinthians 12). The Orthodox Church recognizes these gifts as vital to the life of the Church, although their expression may differ depending on the needs of the Church in different eras. The gifts of the Spirit are most prominently expressed in the Church's liturgical and sacramental life, as well as in the personal spiritual growth of the faithful.

The Second Coming

Orthodox Christians eagerly anticipate the Second Coming of Christ, confessing that He "will come again to judge the living and the dead, and His kingdom will have no end." Rather than engaging in speculative predictions about the end times, the Orthodox Church focuses on preparing for Christ's return by living in a state of spiritual readiness. The emphasis is on repentance, holy living, and remaining faithful to Christ, so that when He returns, His followers may meet Him with confidence. Orthodox preaching reminds the faithful to "abide in Him, that when He appears, we may have confidence and not be ashamed before Him at His coming" (1 John 2:28).

Heaven

In Orthodox theology, heaven is not merely a future state or distant realm; it is the reality of God's presence, which can be experienced even now. Heaven is the place where God's throne resides, and where the saints and angels dwell. Orthodox Christians believe that their true citizenship is in heaven (Philippians 3:20) and that through the Eucharist and the liturgy, they participate in the heavenly worship here on earth. The architecture of Orthodox churches is designed to reflect this reality, with the dome symbolizing the heavens and the icons providing a glimpse into the eternal. At the end of time, heaven will be fully revealed in the new creation, where the faithful will dwell in God's presence forever.

Hell

Orthodox Christianity teaches that hell is a reality for those who reject God's grace and mercy. It is not merely a place of punishment but a state of separation from God, chosen by those who refuse His love. Jesus spoke frequently of hell, describing it as a place of torment and fire, where those who reject Him will face eternal consequences (Mark 9:43-48). Orthodox teaching emphasizes that God's desire is for all to be saved (1 Timothy 2:4), but He respects human freedom, allowing people to choose their eternal destiny. Hell, therefore, is not a punishment imposed by God, but the natural consequence of rejecting His love.

Creation

Orthodox Christians confess that God is the Creator of all things, as stated in the Nicene Creed: "We believe in one God, the Father Almighty, Maker of heaven and earth." Creation is not seen as a random occurrence, but as the purposeful act of a loving God, who brought the universe into being through His Word (John 1:3). While the Bible is not a scientific textbook, it reveals the profound truth that God is the source of all life. Orthodox Christians see science and faith as complementary rather than contradictory, recognizing that all truth ultimately comes from God. Honest scientific inquiry can lead to a greater appreciation of the beauty and order of God's creation.

THINGS TO KNOW FOR A FIRST VISIT TO AN ORTHODOX CHURCH

The Church Building

Orthodox churches are designed with shapes that carry deep mystical and theological significance. One of the most common shapes is rectangular or oblong, resembling a ship. This symbol is rooted in the idea that the Church, guided by Christ as the master helmsman, carries believers safely through the turbulent seas of life—marked by sin and strife—toward the calm harbor of the Kingdom of Heaven. The image of the Church as a ship reflects its role as a vessel of salvation, moving its members through the spiritual challenges of life to eternal safety.

In many cases, Orthodox churches are also constructed in the shape of a cross. This is a powerful reminder that the faithful are saved through the Crucified Christ, and it is through the Cross that Christians are called to bear their sufferings, united with the sacrifice of Jesus. This cross-shaped architecture proclaims that the center of the Orthodox faith is the Paschal mystery—the death and resurrection of Christ.

Orientation is another crucial element in Orthodox church design. Orthodox churches are traditionally oriented east to west, with the main entrance located at the western end. This eastward orientation holds profound symbolism, representing the transition from the darkness of sin (symbolized by the west) into the light of truth (symbolized by the east). In Orthodox tradition, the east is associated with Christ, who is referred to as the "Light of the

World" and whose return at the Second Coming is anticipated from the east.

On the rooftops of Orthodox churches, one or more cupolas or domes are typically present. In Russian Orthodox architecture, these domes are often onion-shaped, a design intended to resemble the flame of a candle. The flame imagery emphasizes the church's role in lifting prayers and worship upwards toward heaven, symbolizing the constant burning of faith, rising toward God.

Each cupola is topped with a Cross, the ultimate symbol of Christian salvation. In the Russian Orthodox Church, the most frequently seen is the three-bar Cross.[4] This Cross includes the standard horizontal beam to which Christ's hands were nailed, a shorter upper beam, which traditionally held the inscription "Jesus of Nazareth, King of the Jews" (John 19:19), and a slanted lower beam. This slanted bar has unique symbolism: it points upward on one side, signifying the Good Thief who repented and was promised Paradise by Christ (Luke 23:39-43), while the downward angle represents the unrepentant thief, whose path led to Hades. The slanted crossbeam is a particularly Russian feature, and while its exact origins are unclear, it serves to remind the faithful of the

---

[4] **The three-bar cross**, often associated with the Russian Orthodox Church, actually originates from Byzantine tradition, not from Russia. While the Russian Church played a significant role in popularizing and standardizing this cross form, its roots lie in earlier Byzantine Christian practices. This historical connection can be observed in various artifacts, including altar crosses found in the monasteries on Mount Athos, which have preserved many ancient Byzantine liturgical customs and symbols. The three-bar cross thus stands as a testament to the shared heritage between Byzantine and Russian Orthodox traditions, illustrating the continuity and reverence for ancient Christian symbolism that transcends regional distinctions within the Orthodox Church.

profound choice each person faces in life—between repentance and rebellion.

The interior of an Orthodox church is meticulously designed to reflect the sacred truths of the faith, each part symbolizing a spiritual reality. The first area a visitor encounters is the Narthex, also known as the Vestibule, Lity (Greek), or Pritvor (Russian). In ancient times, the Narthex served as a space where Catechumens—those preparing for Baptism—received instruction. It was also where Penitents, who were temporarily excluded from Holy Communion, stood during services. Today, this area still retains its symbolic function, representing the entrance into the life of the Church.

The central part of the church is the Nave, the large open area where the congregation gathers for worship. The Nave is separated from the Sanctuary (Altar) by an Iconostasis—a screen or wall adorned with icons and doors. This partition emphasizes the mystery of God and the holiness of the Altar, where the Divine Liturgy is celebrated. The Nave is also adorned with icons and murals, each depicting biblical scenes, Christ, the Theotokos (Mother of God), and the Saints. These icons are not mere decorations; they are venerated by the faithful, who light candles and pray before them as part of their worship.

A unique feature of traditional Orthodox churches is the absence of pews. This open space allows worshippers to stand, bow, and perform prostrations freely during services, which is seen as an integral expression of reverence and participation in the liturgy. Standing during worship is an ancient practice that reflects respect for the divine presence.

At the eastern end of the church is the Sanctuary, or Altar, which is reserved for clergy and those assisting in the service. It is separated from the rest of the church by the Iconostasis, a feature that not only symbolizes the veil between heaven and earth but also serves as a visible reminder of the heavenly reality that the church represents.

Byzantine influence in Orthodox church architecture is evident across the regions where Orthodoxy took root, each adapting the style to their local conditions and cultural contexts. In Serbia, for example, the "Rascian"[5] style was dominant until the 14th century. This architectural style is characterized by a series of domed bays along a single axis, with an optional tower over the narthex. Bulgarian church architecture often employed a long, barrel-vaulted or domed structure, typically without internal freestanding supports, making the interiors open and spacious.

Russia, on the other hand, developed the iconic "onion" domes by the 13th century. These domes are practical as they shed snow easily and prevent buildup, especially at the seam between the dome and the supporting drum. This distinctive feature, along with other church designs like the "tent" church, illustrates how native architectural traditions evolved to meet the challenges of the environment. In tent churches, tall steeples rise over a central chamber, their silhouette dramatically contrasting with Russia's

---

[5] **Rascian**: A historical term used primarily in medieval and early modern sources to refer to Serbs. The name derives from "Ras," the early medieval Serbian state and ecclesiastical center. Commonly used by neighboring nations, including Hungarians and Venetians, the term "Rascian" identified Serbs living in regions such as Hungary, Dalmatia, and the Habsburg Monarchy. Though largely outdated, the term reflects historical perceptions of Serbian identity and its connection to the Ras region.

flat landscape. The famous St. Basil's Cathedral in Moscow's Red Square (officially known as the Cathedral of the Intercession of the Most Holy Theotokos on the Moat, or Pokrovsky Cathedral), a collection of nine separate churches, is a striking example of this style.

Romanian Orthodox churches, particularly monastery churches, are recognized for their long, narrow designs, single apses, and roofs with generous overhangs. These churches are also known for their richly painted exteriors, illustrating Biblical scenes and saints. While each region's churches display unique characteristics, a common thread runs through Orthodox architecture—a "family resemblance" built upon Byzantine foundations. Most Orthodox churches feature vaulted ceilings, creating a "celestial" space, and interiors adorned with extensive frescoes or mosaics. Sculptural elements are generally minimal, allowing the flat surfaces to serve as canvases for holy images.

Christian art, as we know it today, began to take shape around the late second or early third century. However, the Orthodox Church teaches that the use of images in worship is rooted in apostolic tradition. According to Orthodox belief, the first icons of Christ and the Virgin Mary were created by St. Luke, and the first image of Christ, the Mandylion (The Savior Not Made by Hands, Image of Edessa, Acheiropoieta), was imprinted by Christ Himself on a cloth. This image was later enshrined in Edessa and became a prototype for future representations of Christ.

One of the most striking aspects of an Orthodox church is the prominence of Holy Icons. The Iconostasis, walls, and ceilings are often covered with icons and murals. These images are central to

Orthodox worship, with the faithful kissing icons, lighting candles before them, and offering prayers. Icons are censed by the clergy and carried in processions during major feasts, reflecting their integral role in the Church's liturgical life.

Many who are unfamiliar with Orthodox practice may wonder about the significance of these actions. Icons are not idols, nor are they worshipped in and of themselves. Instead, they are windows into heaven, revealing the spiritual reality they depict. The Orthodox tradition of venerating icons is deeply rooted in the doctrine of the Incarnation of Christ. Since the Son of God took on human flesh and made the invisible God visible, it became possible to depict Him. As St. John the Evangelist teaches, "The Word became flesh and dwelt among us" (John 1:14), making the divine image visible in Christ.

St. John of Damascus,[6] one of the great defenders of icons during the iconoclastic controversies of the 8th century, explained that because Christ became man, we can now depict Him. Through icons, we contemplate the divine in visible form. Icons are not merely religious art but are theological images that convey the truths of the Christian faith.

---

[6] **St. John of Damascus**: An 8th-century monk, priest, and theologian (ca. 675–749), renowned as one of the greatest Church Fathers and defenders of Orthodox Christianity. Born in Damascus and later becoming a monk at the Monastery of St. Sabbas near Jerusalem, St. John is celebrated for his defense of the veneration of icons during the Iconoclastic Controversy. His most notable works include The Fount of Knowledge, a comprehensive theological treatise, and numerous hymns still used in Orthodox liturgical services. St. John is also regarded as one of the last great Greek theologians of the patristic era. His feast day is celebrated on December 4th / December 17th.

The 7th Ecumenical Council affirmed the use of icons in worship, teaching that they complement and clarify the truths of Holy Scripture. Icons and Scripture together form a complete expression of the faith, as stated in the Council's decrees: "If the Icon is shown by Holy Scripture, Holy Scripture is made incontestably clear by the Icon."

Icons of Christ, the Theotokos, and the Saints are venerated not because of the materials used to create them—wood, paint, or gold—but because they depict the holy persons they represent. When Orthodox Christians venerate an icon, they are expressing honor and reverence for the one depicted, offering worship to God alone through these holy images.

As St. Basil the Great[7] explains, "We venerate the material objects through which our salvation is effected"—whether it is the Cross, the Gospel, the relics of Saints, or icons. Through these sacred images, the faithful are reminded of Christ's Incarnation and the Saints' participation in God's glory. Icons of Saints act as meeting points between the faithful on earth (the Church Militant) and the Saints in heaven (the Church Triumphant), reminding believers that the Saints are not distant figures of the past, but living, active intercessors before God.

---

[7] **St. Basil the Great**: A 4th-century bishop, theologian, and Church Father (ca. 330–379), revered for his contributions to Christian theology, monasticism, and liturgical practice. As the Archbishop of Caesarea in Cappadocia, St. Basil defended the Nicene faith against Arianism and played a key role in shaping Trinitarian doctrine. His writings, including On the Holy Spirit and The Hexaemeron, remain foundational to Christian theology. St. Basil also established guidelines for communal monastic life, influencing Eastern monasticism for centuries. He is credited with contributions to the Divine Liturgy that bears his name. His feast day is celebrated on January 1st / January 14th.

The Iconostasis itself is a prominent feature of the Orthodox church. It consists of multiple rows of icons, with the central portion broken by the Royal Doors and the Deacon's Doors. The Royal Doors often display icons of the Annunciation and the four Evangelists, symbolizing the proclamation of the Good News of Christ's coming. Above the Royal Doors is often an icon of the Mystical Supper, reflecting the ongoing celebration of the Holy Eucharist in the Altar beyond.

To the right of the Royal Doors is the icon of Christ, and to the left, an icon of the Theotokos. On the Deacon's Doors, one often finds images of angelic figures or saintly deacons, representing the heavenly and earthly ministers of God's altar. In some churches, icons of particular local significance are placed on the lower tier of the Iconostasis, known as the Local Icons.

Ascending above these, the Deisis tier includes icons of Christ, the Theotokos, and St. John the Forerunner (John the Baptist), surrounded by various saints, all depicted as offering prayers to Christ. This tier emphasizes the intercessory role of the Saints. Above this, a row of icons depicts the Feasts of the Church, highlighting key events in the life of Christ and the Theotokos. The highest tier typically features the Old Testament Prophets, with an icon of the Theotokos holding the Christ Child at the center, symbolizing the fulfillment of their prophecies.

At the pinnacle of the Iconostasis stands the Cross, the ultimate symbol of Christ's victory over death and the means of our salvation.

Beyond the Iconostasis lies the Altar (Sanctuary), which is set apart for those serving the Divine Liturgy. This sacred space

Discovering Orthodox Christianity

represents both the throne of God and the tomb of Christ, with the Holy Table as its central feature. The Holy Table is square in shape, draped in two coverings: a white linen cloth representing Christ's burial shroud, and an ornate outer cloth symbolizing the glory of God's throne. On the Holy Table, the Holy Gifts—the bread and wine that will become the Body and Blood of Christ—are consecrated.

The Altar is a place of mystery and reverence, where the Church's most profound acts of worship take place, and only those who are consecrated to serve in the liturgy may enter.

When you enter an Orthodox church, you may notice what seems like a flurry of activity—people walking up to the front, praying in front of the iconostasis, lighting candles, making the sign of the cross, and kissing icons, all while the service is already underway. You might wonder, "Where do I stand? What is going on? Am I late?" The service seems to have started long before the posted time of 7:30 or 9:30. But don't worry—this is a common experience in Orthodox worship and highlights the dynamic, living nature of the faith.

Orthodox services are fluid, starting with preparatory prayers like the Hours and Matins (Orthros)[8] before the Divine Liturgy itself. These services are not isolated events but flow into one another

---

[8] **Hours and Matins (Orthros)**: Liturgical services within the daily cycle of Orthodox Christian worship. The Hours—First, Third, Sixth, and Ninth—are short services that include psalms, hymns, and prayers, marking the sanctification of time throughout the day. Matins (Orthros), often referred to as the morning service, is celebrated in the early hours before sunrise and is one of the most elaborate services, featuring psalm readings, hymns, canons, and the Gospel. Both services aim to orient the faithful toward God, offering continual praise and reflection on the life of Christ and the saints.

seamlessly, creating a tapestry of continual prayer and worship that can often last for three hours or more. The times are approximate, and the services build on each other, invoking a sense of timelessness that reflects the eternal nature of the Kingdom of Heaven. As Fr. Victor Potapov described it, the priest "stands in the flame" at the altar, symbolizing the unceasing offering of prayer before God.

The atmosphere in an Orthodox church can feel both structured and organic. Worshippers come and go with reverence, arriving at different times—some during Matins, others as the Liturgy is already in progress. In some traditions, it is common to enter the church, light a candle, venerate the icons, and find a place for prayer even if the service has already begun. This practice is not seen as disruptive but as an expression of personal devotion, where each person enters into the flow of communal worship at their own pace.

Candles, for instance, are not merely symbolic but are physical prayers offered up to God. The lighting of a candle expresses the believer's prayers, hopes, and intercessions for others, illuminating their faith in the presence of God and the saints. The kissing of icons, likewise, reflects the deep connection Orthodox Christians have with the holy figures depicted, embodying the love and veneration that transcends time and space.

Despite what might appear to an outsider as a chaotic or unstructured environment, the heart of Orthodox worship is deeply communal and purposeful. The church is not just a building, but a place where heaven and earth meet, where the visible and invisible worlds come together in a mystical union.

Worship is both an individual and collective offering, a continuous dialogue with God. Punctuality is valued, but it is not the ultimate focus—what matters most is the sincerity and depth of each person's prayer and connection to God. The perceived "commotion" is, in fact, the heartbeat of a living, breathing faith that invites every soul to participate in the eternal worship of God.

Stand Up, Stand Up for Jesus

In the Orthodox tradition, the faithful stand for nearly the entire service. Some churches may not have any chairs at all, while others—especially those using pre-existing church buildings—might have pews. This practice of standing dates back to the early Church and reflects the posture of attentiveness and reverence in the presence of God. Standing is considered the appropriate posture for prayer, symbolizing the Resurrection and the human spirit standing before the Almighty in alertness and respect.

If standing is difficult, feel free to sit; no one should judge or mind. In most Orthodox parishes, there are no strict rules regarding sitting or standing, and the faithful are encouraged to participate in worship to the best of their ability. For the elderly, the infirm, or those with physical limitations, chairs or pews are provided, and it is common to see people alternate between standing and sitting as needed.

Over time, standing becomes easier, and for many, it deepens the sense of reverence in worship. In fact, many find that standing helps cultivate a prayerful mindset, as it keeps the body engaged and attentive, preventing distractions. The act of standing is not just a physical posture but a spiritual one, echoing the tradition of the saints who stood in constant prayer and vigilance before God.

As St. Basil the Great reminds us, standing during prayer is a reminder of Christ's Resurrection, and by doing so, we participate in the new life He has given us.

Additionally, the communal nature of standing in worship unites the faithful in a common gesture of humility and devotion. Standing side by side with fellow believers reminds us that we are part of the Body of Christ, gathered together not as spectators but as active participants in the heavenly liturgy. This sense of unity is further expressed during specific moments of the service, such as when the congregation stands during the reading of the Gospel, the Great Entrance, or the consecration of the Holy Gifts.

Ultimately, the posture of standing, like other aspects of Orthodox worship, serves as a physical expression of our inner reverence and love for God. While the outward form is important, what truly matters is the intention and heart behind the action. Whether standing or sitting, the Orthodox Church invites each worshipper to engage fully in the sacred mystery unfolding before them.

Sign of the Cross

Orthodox Christians frequently make the sign of the cross, a gesture that is both an outward expression of faith and a powerful reminder of the central mysteries of Christianity. This is done whenever the Holy Trinity is invoked, during veneration of the cross or icons, and at various points throughout the Liturgy, particularly during prayers, blessings, and hymns. The sign of the cross is more than a simple ritual—it is an embodied prayer, calling upon the name of the Father, the Son, and the Holy Spirit, while uniting mind, body, and spirit in worship.

The faithful cross themselves from right to left, a practice that dates back centuries and is followed by the Eastern Orthodox tradition. The specific hand posture also holds deep theological meaning: the thumb and first two fingers pressed together symbolize the Holy Trinity—Father, Son, and Holy Spirit. The last two fingers folded down represent the two natures of Christ, fully divine and fully human. Together, this hand formation expresses a confession of faith in the Incarnation and the Trinity, two of the most fundamental doctrines of Orthodox Christianity.

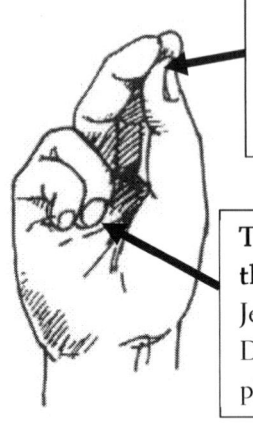

With the Right hand, place the Thumb, First and Second finger together. This represents the Holy Trinity: God the Father, God the Son and God the Holy Spirit - **One God.**

The last two fingers are placed to the palm of the hand. This represents the two natures of Jesus Christ, both fully human and fully Divine, who came down to earth (2 fingers placed in palm) for the salvation of mankind.

While it may seem confusing at first for those new to the Orthodox Church, there is no need to worry about getting the gesture wrong. What truly matters is the heart behind the action—the sincerity of one's prayer and devotion. Over time, this sacred gesture will become second nature, serving as a constant reminder of God's presence and protection in daily life. As St. John Chrysostom once taught, "*Let us not make the sign of the Cross with a careless hand, but as soldiers prepare for battle, let us form it with attention, invoking the name of Christ."*

Picture by Fr. Anthony Alevizopoulos

Beyond its liturgical use, the sign of the cross is also a personal act of devotion and protection. Orthodox Christians make the sign of the cross when they pray at home, before and after meals, upon waking up, before going to sleep, and during moments of temptation or danger. This action is not merely a symbol but a proclamation of faith and a call for divine help, protection, and blessing. It is believed that the sign of the cross has the power to ward off evil and draw the grace of God into one's life.

In fact, the cross itself is revered as the ultimate sign of victory over death and sin, and by making the sign of the cross, believers unite themselves to Christ's sacrifice and resurrection. Through this simple yet profound gesture, Orthodox Christians continually reaffirm their faith and trust in God's saving power, connecting their daily lives with the sacred mystery of salvation.

Clergy Etiquette

When greeting Orthodox clergy in person, a respectful protocol is followed to honor their role within the Church. Deacons and priests are addressed as "Father," while bishops are addressed as "Your Grace," and higher-ranking bishops, such as Metropolitans or Archbishops, are referred to as "Your Eminence." Patriarchs are called "Your Beatitude." When approaching a priest or bishop, it is customary to ask for a blessing by bowing, touching the floor with the right hand, placing the right hand over the left (palms upward), and saying, "Bless, Father" (or "Bless, Your Grace," "Your Eminence," etc.). The clergy member responds with "May the Lord bless you" and makes the Sign of the Cross, after which the faithful kiss the cleric's hand as a sign of respect for his apostolic office and his handling of the Holy Mysteries during the Divine Liturgy.

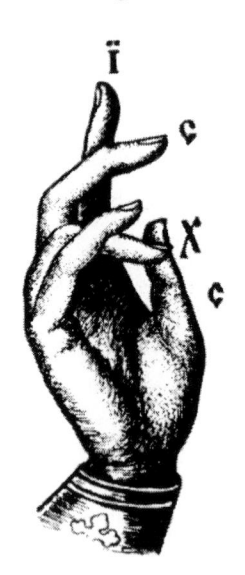

The blessing conferred by a priest or bishop is made with the formation of the Christogram "ICXC," representing the abbreviation of "Jesus Christ" in Greek. The tradition of asking for blessings and kissing the hand of clergy underscores the reverence Orthodox Christians hold for the sacraments, especially the Eucharist. As Saint John Chrysostom emphasized, the hands of a priest are honored because they have touched the Body and Blood of Christ during the Liturgy.

For married clergy, their wives also receive titles of respect. In Greek, the priest's wife is called "Presbytera," in Russian, "Matushka," in Serbian, "Papadiya," and in Ukrainian, "Panimatushka" or "Panimatka." The deacon's wife is addressed as "Diakonissa" in Greek, while the Slavic churches often use the same titles for both priests' and deacons' wives. Addressing clergy properly is not only a mark of respect but also reflects the unique spiritual dignity attached to their roles.

When speaking to clergy over the phone or writing letters, it is customary to ask for their blessing. Conversations with a priest begin with "Father, bless," and for a bishop, "Bless, Despota"[9] or "Bless, Your Grace." Letters to clergy also follow this pattern, beginning with "Bless, Father," and concluding with "Kissing your right hand." It is inappropriate for laypeople to offer a blessing to clergy, as the grace to bless comes from the sacrament of Holy Orders.

In formal writing, deacons are addressed as "The Reverend Deacon," or if they are monastic deacons, "The Reverend Hierodeacon." For higher ranks such as Archdeacon or Protodeacon, "The Reverend Archdeacon" or "The Reverend Protodeacon" is used. Priests are formally addressed as "The

---

[9] **Despota** (Despot): A title of honor and authority in the Byzantine tradition, bestowed upon rulers and high-ranking members of the imperial family, often signifying governance over a specific territory or vassal state. In Orthodox Christian usage, it is also employed as a term of respect when addressing hierarchs, particularly bishops, signifying their spiritual authority as overseers of the Church. Rooted in the Byzantine hierarchy, the title embodies both reverence and recognition of divinely entrusted leadership within the Church.

Reverend Father" or "The Reverend Hieromonk" if they are monastic priests, and bishops as "The Right Reverend Bishop," followed by their first name. Archbishops, Metropolitans, and Patriarchs receive the title "The Most Reverend" followed by their rank.

Monastics, regardless of their rank, are called "the Venerable or Father" if male, and "Mother" or "Sister" if female. In the Orthodox Church, "Brother" is neither an official title nor a recognized form of address. Novices entering monastic life are addressed simply by their first names, reflecting their humble position as beginners on the monastic path. Although a novice has taken an initial step towards monastic commitment, this status does not constitute an ecclesiastical rank nor does it carry any formal designation within the Church. Unlike ordained clergy or fully tonsured monks, novices do not hold a distinct title that requires a specific form of address. Their role remains that of a disciple under spiritual guidance, learning the disciplines and practices of monasticism without yet assuming an official position in the ecclesiastical hierarchy. This approach underscores the Orthodox emphasis on humility and gradual spiritual growth, where titles and formalities are reserved for those who have undergone further stages of monastic commitment. An abbot is addressed as "The Very Reverend Abbot," whether he holds priestly rank or not.

In summary, Orthodox tradition emphasizes profound respect for the clergy, their sacred duties, and the mysteries they administer. This respect is reflected in the formal greetings, titles, and customs associated with interacting with clergy. These practices foster reverence for the apostolic succession and the deep spiritual significance of the priesthood in Orthodox life.

Kneeling, Prostrating?

In Orthodox worship, kneeling is rare, but prostration is common, especially during specific moments of repentance and prayer. A prostration involves kneeling and then bowing forward to touch the forehead to the floor in humility before God. This act, reminiscent of ancient Middle Eastern worship practices, may seem unusual to those unfamiliar with it, but it carries profound spiritual significance in the Orthodox tradition.

Prostration is an outward sign of deep inner reverence, symbolizing the worshipper's humility before God and acknowledgment of His majesty and mercy. It is a physical act of submission, representing both the fallenness of humanity and the longing for repentance and forgiveness. In moments of prostration, the worshipper lowers themselves to the earth, only to rise again, symbolizing the human experience of falling into sin and being raised through God's grace. The act also recalls the profound humility of Christ, who "humbled himself, becoming obedient to death, even death on a cross" (Philippians 2:8).

Women may find that full skirts and flat shoes make prostrations easier, though worshippers are encouraged to dress modestly and comfortably, in a manner suitable for the sacred space. Prostration is most commonly practiced during Great Lent, at services such as the Presanctified Liturgy, and during personal prayers of repentance.

While prostration is a significant aspect of Orthodox piety, there is also room for individual expressions of devotion. Some may choose to kneel or simply bow their heads in reverence, while others may stand silently, praying with their hearts. In Orthodox worship, there is a diversity of personal expressions, and the focus is always on the sincerity of one's prayer rather than the exact form of outward gestures. Whether one kneels, bows, or stands, each posture is an offering of love and reverence to God.

It is also worth noting that during certain liturgical seasons, particularly from Pascha (Easter)[10] to Pentecost, prostrations are traditionally not made, as this is a time of celebration and joy in the Resurrection. The absence of prostrations during these periods serves to emphasize the triumph of Christ over death and the new life given to the faithful.

Orthodox worship allows for a range of expressions of piety, without a sense of being judged or watched. Each believer is encouraged to enter into the liturgy with reverence, offering their prayers and worship in a way that feels authentic and meaningful to them.

Act of Kissing

Kissing is a common and deeply meaningful way Orthodox Christians express reverence and love for holy things. It is an ancient tradition rooted in both biblical and early Christian practice, symbolizing devotion, respect, and the shared love of God and neighbor. We kiss icons—kissing Christ on the feet, and saints on the hands—as a sign of veneration and respect,

---

[10] **Pascha**: The Feast of Feasts in Orthodox Christianity, commemorating the Resurrection of our Lord and Savior Jesus Christ from the dead. Pascha, derived from the Hebrew word Pesach (Passover), celebrates Christ's victory over sin and death, fulfilling the Old Testament Passover and granting eternal life to humanity. Observed with great joy and solemnity, it begins with the Paschal Vigil, marked by the proclamation, "Christ is Risen!" (Christos Anesti!) and the response, "Indeed He is Risen!" (Alithos Anesti!). Pascha serves as the central event of the liturgical year, expressing the culmination of Christ's salvific work.

acknowledging their sanctity and their intercession on our behalf. This act connects the faithful not only to the figure depicted but to the deeper spiritual reality behind the image.

Beyond icons, Orthodox Christians also kiss the chalice, the priest's vestments, and the cross at the end of the service. Each kiss is a gesture of devotion, signifying a connection with the holy object or person being venerated. For instance, kissing the chalice shows respect for the Holy Eucharist, the life-giving Body and Blood of Christ, while kissing the priest's vestments is a recognition of the priest's role as a servant of God, entrusted with administering the sacraments.

An important aspect of this practice is that it is not meant to be formal or distant; it reflects the closeness of the community and our shared faith. In Orthodox liturgical tradition, the "kiss of peace" is not merely an exchange of "peace" but a profound acknowledgment of the presence of Christ and a shared commitment to the faith, which is about to be proclaimed in the Creed. While a version of the kiss of peace existed in ancient liturgical texts, it is now practiced exclusively within the altar by the clergy. In some Orthodox communities today, particularly among Antiochians, this practice has seen a modern revival, although it is not common across all jurisdictions.

Among Old Rite Russian Orthodox, a similar gesture occurs, though not within the context of the Divine Liturgy, but rather when receiving a blessing from the priest.

It is worth noting that certain modern liturgical adaptations seen in some Orthodox communities—often influenced by a form of "liturgical archaeology"—can be based on assumptions rather than long-standing tradition. For example, reintroducing practices like deaconesses or Communion in the hand may seem like historical restoration but lack an established place in contemporary Orthodox worship. Many practices, while historically present, have faded over time due to the Church's wisdom and discretion, evolving to meet the spiritual needs of the faithful within the context of the Church's living tradition.

This physical expression of veneration reminds us that our faith is incarnational—that it involves both body and soul, and that every aspect of our being is called to participate in the worship of God. The act of kissing, much like making the sign of the cross, is an embodied prayer, one that brings the believer closer to the sacred.

For many, these gestures may seem unusual at first, especially if they are unfamiliar with Orthodox customs. However, the sincerity of these actions is what matters most, not their precision or formality. Over time, these expressions of faith become second nature, deepening one's connection to the Divine and to the wider community of believers.

Blessed Bread and Consecrated Bread

Only Orthodox Christians may partake in Communion, as it represents a deeper commitment to the faith, the Church, and a shared confession of belief. Communion, or the Eucharist, is not just a symbolic meal but is considered the true Body and Blood of Christ. This mystery, known as the "Divine Liturgy," is at the heart of Orthodox Christian life. Participating in the Eucharist is a profound spiritual act, a moment when the faithful unite with Christ and each other in a sacred bond.

The Eucharist, in the Orthodox Church, is treated with profound reverence. The faithful prepare by fasting from food and drink from midnight before receiving Communion. This fast is seen as a spiritual exercise that helps purify both body and soul, preparing the heart to receive Christ. It is not a punishment or burden but rather an act of self-discipline that aligns the believer's heart with the holy and sacred mystery of the Eucharist. As St. John Chrysostom once said, "Fasting is the support of our soul: it gives us wings to ascend on high, and to enjoy the highest contemplation."

Fasting before Communion is also accompanied by prayer and self-reflection, especially in the days leading up to Sunday or feast day liturgies. The faithful are encouraged to participate in the sacrament of Confession beforehand, seeking reconciliation with God and their neighbor. This personal preparation highlights the seriousness and depth of receiving Communion, which is seen not as a casual act but as an encounter with the living God. As the prayers before Communion emphasize, "Let us draw near in faith and love, that we may become partakers of life eternal."

The practice of receiving the Eucharist within the Orthodox Church is a reminder of Christ's words at the Last Supper: "Take, eat; this is My Body... Drink of it, all of you; this is My Blood of the New Covenant" (Matthew 26:26-28). For Orthodox Christians, these words are taken quite literally, as the bread and wine are believed to be transformed into Christ's Body and Blood through the invocation of the Holy Spirit during the Divine Liturgy. The experience of Communion is not merely symbolic but a true participation in the life and grace of Christ.

While the Eucharist is reserved for Orthodox Christians, the Church warmly invites all to witness and experience the beauty of the Liturgy. Antidoron, a term that means "in place of the Gifts," refers specifically to the portions cut from the sides of the Lamb—the central piece of bread consecrated during the Divine Liturgy. It is not the same as the general blessed bread distributed to the faithful at the end of the service, which is typically cut-up prosphora.

In the Russian Orthodox tradition, the pieces of antidoron taken from the Lamb are small and generally suffice only for the clergy's *zapivka*,[11] or post-Communion wine and water, unless the prosphora used is large enough to allow for distribution to the congregation, as is often the case in the Greek Orthodox practice.

For this reason, antidoron from the Lamb should not be given to non-Orthodox attendees, as it holds particular significance for those within the Orthodox faith. It serves as a spiritual substitute for those who, for reasons such as lack of preparation or a penance, do not partake in Holy Communion on that occasion.

Providing non-Orthodox with blessed bread from other prosphora can be an act of *economia*—a pastoral concession or act of condescension intended to welcome visitors. However, this is not considered a canonical practice and should not be mistaken for an endorsement of general participation in liturgical elements reserved for Orthodox faithful. Proper understanding and respect

---

[11] **Zapivka** is the ritual act of drinking a small amount of wine mixed with water after receiving Holy Communion to cleanse the mouth and complete the Eucharistic.

for the distinction between antidoron and general blessed bread help maintain the sacramental integrity of Orthodox worship.

Where's the General Confession?

Orthodox Christians confess their sins privately to their priest, rather than in a general confession during the Liturgy. This sacrament of Confession, also called *Holy Repentance*, is an essential part of Orthodox spiritual life, where the believer acknowledges their sins and receives absolution. The priest acts as a spiritual father, offering guidance, encouragement, and the grace of forgiveness through the prayer of absolution. The priest does not act on his own but represents Christ, to whom the confession is ultimately offered. As St. John Climacus[12] wrote in *The Ladder of Divine Ascent*, "Confession is a spiritual rebirth and a return to God."

During Confession, the priest may offer advice or guidance to help the person in their spiritual journey, offering support as they work toward spiritual healing and transformation. It is not only about recounting one's sins but also seeking help and direction to live a more faithful Christian life. As a spiritual father, the priest builds a relationship of trust with his parishioners, helping them to understand how to overcome struggles and grow in faith.

---

[12] **St. John Climacus**: A 6th–7th-century Orthodox monk, ascetic, and abbot of St. Catherine's Monastery on Mount Sinai, best known for his spiritual treatise, The Ladder of Divine Ascent. This seminal work, written as a guide for monastic and lay Christians, outlines a 30-step path toward spiritual perfection, symbolizing the ladder Jacob saw in his vision (Genesis 28:12). Each step addresses specific virtues and vices, offering practical wisdom for overcoming passions and attaining union with God. St. John, also known as "John of the Ladder," is commemorated on the Fourth Sunday of Great Lent and on March 30th / April 12th.

Orthodox Confession emphasizes not only forgiveness but the restoration of the soul through Christ's grace.

The Role of the Priest's Wife

The role of the priest's wife is also highly respected within the Orthodox community, and she is often addressed by a special title depending on the cultural tradition. In Arabic, she is called *Khouria*; in Greek, *Presbytera*; and in Russian, *Matushka*, meaning "priest's wife" or "mother." These titles reflect her position as both a support to her husband in his ministry and a spiritual mother to the community. While not ordained, she often plays an important role in parish life, providing counsel, organizing community events, and helping to create a warm and welcoming church atmosphere.

In many Orthodox traditions, the priest's wife is viewed as a partner in the priest's ministry. Although her role may vary depending on the parish or cultural context, she is often seen as a figure of wisdom, care, and hospitality. The priest and his wife together often model a Christian family, providing an example of faith and devotion to their congregation. They both bear the responsibility of supporting the spiritual growth of their community, with the priest leading in the sacraments and the *Matushka*, *Presbytera*, or *Khouria* often offering more personal, behind-the-scenes guidance and support.

Together, the priest and his wife embody the Christian ideal of service and humility. While the priest administers the sacraments, the priest's wife often acts as a source of comfort and strength for the parish, especially to women and families. This partnership reflects the unity and cooperation that are central to Orthodox

Christian life, where the entire Church functions as one body in Christ.

Singing and Chanting

Orthodox worship is filled with music—approximately 75% of the service is sung, a tradition that creates a prayerful atmosphere and reflects the belief that worship should be a harmonious offering to God. The use of *a cappella* singing, without instruments, is a hallmark of Orthodox worship. This ancient practice emphasizes the purity of the human voice, which, as the Church Fathers taught, is the instrument created by God for the purpose of praising Him.

Traditionally, no instruments are used; instead, the congregation and choir sing together, creating a rich, layered sound that fills the church. The chanting and hymns are often antiphonal, meaning the choir and congregation alternate verses, or the choir may sing responses to the priest's prayers. This communal singing draws the faithful into the liturgical action, uniting them in worship as one voice offering praise to God. As St. John Chrysostom said, "Nothing uplifts the soul and enables it to approach God more than musical sounds, skillfully combined."

For those unfamiliar with the tradition, the constant singing can feel overwhelming at first, especially if they are new to the flow of Orthodox services. However, the structure and repetition of the hymns quickly become familiar, and soon you'll find yourself joining in. The melodies are often simple yet profound, designed to be easily learned by the congregation over time. The music remains largely the same from week to week, allowing the prayers and hymns to sink deeply into your heart and mind.

The unchanging nature of many hymns, especially during certain liturgical seasons, helps create a spiritual rhythm, grounding the faithful in the timeless truths of the faith. The Cherubic Hymn, for instance, sung during the Great Entrance, invites the congregation to "lay aside all earthly cares" as they mystically participate in the heavenly worship of angels. Similarly, the Trisagion Hymn ("Holy God, Holy Mighty, Holy Immortal, have mercy on us") is a prayer of praise that has been sung in the Church for centuries, connecting today's worshippers with generations of Christians before them.

The beauty of Orthodox music lies not only in its sound but in its theological depth. The hymns of the Church are filled with scriptural references, teachings of the saints, and theological insights, making the music not just an accompaniment to worship but a form of teaching and prayer in itself. For example, during Great Lent,[13] the Lenten Triodion contains hymns that guide the faithful through themes of repentance and forgiveness, preparing their hearts for the celebration of Pascha (Easter).

The lack of instruments also reflects the Orthodox emphasis on simplicity and focus during worship. By using only the human voice, the Church underscores the idea that it is the heart and soul that matter most in prayer, not external adornments. This simplicity allows worshippers to enter more deeply into the

---

[13] **Great Lent**: The forty-day period of fasting, prayer, and repentance in the Orthodox Church, preceding Holy Week and Pascha. Also known as the "Great Fast," it mirrors Christ's forty days of fasting in the wilderness and is a time for spiritual renewal, self-discipline, and preparation for the celebration of the Resurrection. Great Lent begins on Clean Monday and is marked by liturgical services such as the Great Canon of St. Andrew of Crete, the Presanctified Liturgy, and an emphasis on almsgiving and confession. It culminates in Lazarus Saturday and Palm Sunday, leading into Holy Week.

spiritual mysteries being celebrated, with the music serving as a vehicle for prayer, not a distraction.

Over time, the melodies, tones, and prayers sung in Orthodox services become part of the worshipper's inner life, offering comfort, strength, and spiritual insight. As the psalms remind us, "Sing praises to the Lord, for He has done gloriously" (Isaiah 12:5). Through the power of music, Orthodox worship invites every participant into the eternal song of praise that echoes in the heavens.

The Timeless Rhythm of Orthodox Liturgy

Orthodox worship doesn't rush. Even when the priest or deacon intones, "Let us complete our prayer to the Lord," it's not a signal that the service is about to end quickly. Expect a bit more time before the conclusion, as Orthodox worship is designed to be an unhurried experience of communion with God. The phrase, often heard during the Divine Liturgy, is a reminder that prayer is not simply a task to be completed, but a continual offering to God. This phrase marks the beginning of the final section of the Liturgy, but still includes important prayers and blessings. It is a call for the faithful to remain attentive and prayerful as the service draws to its conclusion. In Orthodox worship, the culmination of the Liturgy is just as significant as its beginning, and every moment is filled with spiritual meaning.

Historically, the original Liturgy in the early Church lasted over five hours, and though it has been shortened today, the Orthodox liturgical services still invite the faithful to dwell in the presence of God without the pressures of time. There is no rush to finish, as the emphasis is on fully engaging with the sacred mysteries

Discovering Orthodox Christianity

unfolding in the service. As St. Gregory the Theologian[14] once said, "Nothing done in haste can be done well." Orthodox worship embodies this principle, offering time and space for reflection, prayer, and communion with God.

One of the most beautiful aspects of the Divine Liturgy is its ability to draw the worshipper into a sense of timelessness, where earthly concerns fall away, and the heart and mind are fully focused on God. The hymns, prayers, and readings unfold in a deliberate, rhythmic pattern that allows for deep contemplation and immersion in the worship experience. This unhurried pace is intentional, designed to engage both heart and mind, drawing the faithful closer to God through reverent and patient worship.

The Divine Liturgy, while shorter than in ancient times, still retains its profound sense of sacred time. Every movement, word, and chant is imbued with meaning, and nothing is hurried. The faithful are invited to participate in this timeless rhythm, to step outside the busyness of daily life and enter into the eternal worship of the heavenly kingdom. As St. John of Kronstadt[15] observed,

---

[14] **St. Gregory the Theologian**: A 4th-century Archbishop of Constantinople (ca. 329–390) and one of the greatest theologians of the Orthodox Church, renowned for his eloquence and profound teachings on the Holy Trinity. Born in Nazianzus, Cappadocia, he was a close friend of St. Basil the Great and a defender of the Nicene faith against Arianism. His Five Theological Orations are masterpieces of Orthodox theology, articulating the doctrine of the Trinity with clarity and depth. St. Gregory is one of the Three Holy Hierarchs, alongside St. Basil the Great and St. John Chrysostom. He is commemorated on January 25th / February 7th.

[15] **St. John of Kronstadt**: A 19th-century Russian Orthodox priest and wonderworker (1829–1908), known for his deep faith, pastoral care, and numerous miracles. Serving as a parish priest at St. Andrew's Cathedral in Kronstadt, he revitalized spiritual life through his powerful sermons, charitable works, and establishment of philanthropic institutions. His renowned work, My Life in Christ, reflects his profound spiritual insights and practical guidance for

"The Church is heaven on earth, where the eternal and the temporal meet." In this way, Orthodox worship serves as a bridge between the earthly and the divine, and it is through this slow, intentional worship that the faithful experience God's presence more fully.

For those new to Orthodox services, the slower pace can be surprising. In a world that often values speed and efficiency, the Liturgy's length and deliberateness can feel countercultural. However, over time, this unhurried worship becomes a welcome reprieve, allowing the soul to breathe and the mind to rest in the peace of Christ. Worship is not meant to be rushed or hurried; it is an opportunity to step into God's presence, to listen, pray, and grow in communion with Him.

Ultimately, the timelessness of Orthodox worship reflects the eternal nature of God and invites the faithful to participate in a sacred reality that transcends the temporal world. As the prayers rise, the faithful are lifted into a space where time no longer matters, and the only focus is on worshipping the Creator.

The Divine Liturgy

The word *Liturgy* carries profound historical and theological significance. It originates from the Greek word *leitourgia*, which, in classical times, referred to a public duty performed by citizens for the good of the community. In the Septuagint, the Greek

---

Christian living. St. John's ministry extended across Russia, where he became a spiritual father to thousands. He was glorified as a saint in 1964 by the Russian Orthodox Church Outside of Russia and in 1990 by the Moscow Patriarchate. His feast day is celebrated on October 19th / November 1st and December 20th / January 2nd.

translation of the Old Testament, *leitourgia* was used to describe the worship conducted in the Temple of Jerusalem. Today, for Orthodox Christians, the term has come to signify the public worship of the Church. More than just a ritual or ceremony, the Divine Liturgy is an expression of the communal, corporate action of the people of God—hence why it is often translated as "the work of the people." However, when it is called the *Divine* Liturgy, it signifies that this common action is not just any work but the holy work of God's people. It is the participation in and experience of the Kingdom of God here and now, in the very act of gathering to worship Him.

The Divine Liturgy is not a spectacle performed by clergy while the laity merely watch; it is a communal act of worship, with each baptized believer participating fully as a member of the "royal priesthood... a people belonging to God" (1 Peter 2:9). This highlights an essential aspect of the Liturgy: every person present is called to be an active, conscious participant, co-celebrating with the clergy, not passive spectators. The entire Church—the body of believers—is united in the Liturgy, making it a shared experience of divine grace and the coming of God's Kingdom.

The Divine Liturgy is also known as the *Eucharist*, a term deeply rooted in the Old Testament's Passover meal. This sacred meal commemorated the Israelites' liberation from Egyptian bondage, as described in the Book of Exodus. However, at the Last Supper, Christ transformed this Passover tradition into an act that commemorates His life, death, and resurrection. In the Christian Eucharist, Christ becomes the new and eternal Passover lamb, whose sacrificial death and resurrection free humanity from the bondage of sin, evil, and death. The Eucharist thus becomes an expression of *Eucharistia*, the Greek word for "thanksgiving," embodying the Church's gratitude to God for the salvation and eternal life granted through His Son.

One cannot discuss the Divine Liturgy without mentioning St. John Chrysostom, whose liturgical legacy shapes the Orthodox Church's worship to this day. Born in 347 AD and becoming the Patriarch of Constantinople, St. John was renowned for his eloquent preaching, earning him the title *Chrysostomos*, meaning "golden mouth." His homilies, often met with applause, addressed the corruption of the political and clerical elite while advocating for the poor and disenfranchised. He initiated ministries in Constantinople that fed thousands of people daily, demonstrating the Church's responsibility to care for the vulnerable. His legacy in preaching and pastoral care extends beyond his era, as more than 600 of his homilies have survived, and his treatise *On the Priesthood* continues to be a foundational text for Orthodox seminaries.

It is certain that the central prayer of the Eucharistic anaphora, the prayer of offering and thanksgiving, originated from St. John Chrysostom. His unwavering commitment to the integrity of the Gospel led to his exile and eventual death in 407 AD, yet his final words, "Glory to God for everything," resonate as a testament to his enduring faith. Orthodox Christians honor his memory annually on November 13th.

The Divine Liturgy, by its very nature, transcends the boundaries between heaven and earth. This sacred intersection is powerfully captured in the story of Prince Vladimir the Great (Prince of Novgorod from 970 and Grand Prince of Kiev from 978), who sought the true religion for his people. According to the *Russian Primary Chronicle*, Prince Vladimir's envoys visited Constantinople and, after witnessing the Divine Liturgy at the Church of the Holy Wisdom, returned to report, "We knew not whether we were in heaven or on earth... God dwells there among men." Their encounter with the beauty of Orthodox worship illustrates the profound truth that the Divine Liturgy is a glimpse of God's eternal Kingdom, where heaven meets earth, and believers stand in the presence of the divine.

Participating in the Divine Liturgy, then, is more than fulfilling a religious obligation—it is a profound encounter with the living God. As St. Germanos, the 7th-century Patriarch of Constantinople, described, the Divine Liturgy is "an awesome sacrifice" and "the clear image of heavenly realities." Within this sacred act, the Church becomes "heaven on earth" and resonates with the mysteries of Christ's cross, tomb, and resurrection. To attend the Liturgy prayerfully and receive Holy Communion is to experience the deepest mystery of Christian life—the union of the believer with Christ in His Body and Blood.

The Eucharist, also known as *Thanksgiving*, is the ultimate sacrament of gratitude to God for the gift of salvation through Jesus Christ. In this divine meal, the faithful are nourished with the Body and Blood of Christ, fulfilling the Lord's words: "Those who eat my flesh and drink my blood have eternal life" (John 6:53-56). It is in the Eucharist that Christians participate in the eternal life of God's Kingdom, even as they live in this world.

Before the Divine Liturgy begins, a special service of preparation, called the *proskomede* or *prothesis*, is performed. During this service, the bread and wine, which will become the Body and Blood of Christ, are prepared. The bread, called the *prosphora*, is cut while verses from Isaiah 53, describing the Suffering Servant, are recited. Similarly, as the wine and water are poured into the chalice, verses from John 19, recounting the flow of blood and water from Christ's side, are read. This service of preparation is not only a practical necessity but also a moment of profound intercession. Prayers are offered for the living and the departed, invoking the memory of saints and asking for God's mercy on the faithful.

The structure of the Divine Liturgy itself is divided into two main parts: the *Liturgy of the Catechumens* and the *Liturgy of the Faithful*. The first part, also called the *synaxis* or "gathering," focuses on the proclamation of God's Word. It includes readings from the Scriptures, hymns, prayers, and the sermon. Historically, this part of the service was open to everyone, including catechumens (those preparing for baptism) and non-baptized individuals. The second part, the *Liturgy of the Faithful*, is reserved for the faithful—those baptized into the Orthodox Church—and culminates in the reception of Holy Communion.

In ancient times, the division between these two parts of the service was more pronounced, as catechumens were required to leave before the Eucharist began. Although this practice has evolved, the spiritual significance remains. The Liturgy of the Word instructs and prepares the faithful, while the Liturgy of the Eucharist unites them with Christ through the sacrament of Holy Communion.

The Divine Liturgy is a festive celebration, meant to be attended with joy and thanksgiving. It is the fundamental act of the Church, the very heart of Orthodox Christian life. As we gather to worship, we do so not out of obligation but out of a deep sense of gratitude for all that Christ has done for us. The Liturgy is the ultimate expression of the Church's living faith in Jesus Christ and a manifestation of the Holy Spirit's presence within the community of believers.

Yet, as Orthodox Theologian, Father Thomas Hopko once lamented, the richness of the Orthodox liturgical tradition is often unknown or misunderstood by many. Father Alexander Yelchaninov, writing in exile after the Bolshevik Revolution, emphasized the need for believers to engage fully with the life of the Church. He wrote, "We know little, and in most cases do not try to find out anything about our church services... Christianity is not merely a philosophical system, it is a life, a special way of life."

For those seeking a deeper understanding of the mysteries of the Divine Liturgy and its profound significance, the book ***A Complete Guide to The Divine Liturgy: A Step-by-Step Guide to the Orthodox Liturgy of Saint John Chrysostom*** offers a clear and enriching resource. Co-authored with Antony Balnaves, a Great Schema Monk of the Russian Orthodox Church Outside Russia (ROCOR) who spent many years on Mount Athos, this guide provides thoughtful insights into the sacred rites and traditions of Orthodox Christian worship, making it an invaluable companion for both clergy and laity.

The Three Doors

Orthodox churches are distinguished by the iconostasis, a wall of icons that separates the altar (the sanctuary) from the nave, the main area where the congregation gathers. This beautifully adorned barrier is far more than just a decorative partition; it serves as a profound theological statement about the relationship between heaven and earth. The iconostasis visually represents the division between the divine and human realms, yet also emphasizes the connection between them, particularly through the sacrament of the Eucharist.

The central doors of the iconostasis, known as the Holy Doors (or Royal Doors), are used only by the clergy, as they carry the Eucharist through these doors. These doors are often inscribed or decorated with icons of the Annunciation or the four Evangelists, symbolizing the Good News of Christ's incarnation and the opening of the way to salvation. The Holy Doors are opened and closed at specific times during the Divine Liturgy, marking the moments when heaven and earth are mystically united through the prayers and sacraments.

To the sides of the Holy Doors are the Deacon's Doors (or Angel Doors), which are used by the deacons and other altar servers to move between the sanctuary and the nave. These doors often bear icons of deacons or angels, symbolizing their role as servants and messengers of God. The deacons assist in the liturgical actions, but like the Holy Doors, the Deacon's Doors are sacred and signify the passage between the earthly and heavenly realms.

The iconostasis itself is a spiritual bridge, reminding the faithful that while heaven and earth may seem separated, the Eucharist brings them together in Christ. The icons displayed on the iconostasis are not mere decorations; they are windows into the divine, depicting Christ, the Theotokos (Mother of God), and various saints who intercede on behalf of the Church. Most prominently, the icon of Christ is placed to the right of the Holy Doors, while the icon of the Theotokos is placed to the left. This arrangement visually reinforces the centrality of Christ in Orthodox worship, with His mother, the saints, and the angels serving as witnesses to His salvific work.

The iconostasis thus serves as a theological and liturgical focal point, drawing the faithful into the mystery of the Eucharist. It emphasizes that, through Christ's Incarnation, the separation between God and humanity has been bridged, and in every Divine Liturgy, the faithful are invited to participate in the heavenly worship alongside the saints and angels. As St. John of Damascus said, "Icons, in their silence, speak of the spiritual mysteries of the kingdom of God."

In this way, the iconostasis not only marks a physical boundary but also serves as a visual and spiritual invitation. When the Holy Doors open during the Liturgy, they symbolize the opening of the heavens, allowing the faithful a glimpse of the divine mystery that is taking place at the altar. The Eucharist, the pinnacle of the Liturgy, is the ultimate point at which heaven and earth meet, and the iconostasis helps prepare the hearts and minds of the faithful for this sacred encounter.

For those new to Orthodox worship, the iconostasis may seem like a barrier, but in reality, it is a passageway into the divine presence. The icons displayed on the iconostasis serve as reminders of the great cloud of witnesses that surrounds the faithful, interceding on their behalf and inviting them to draw closer to God. Each element of the iconostasis—from the arrangement of the icons to the opening and closing of the Holy Doors—points to the deeper truths of the Orthodox faith: that God became man so that humanity might partake in His divine life.

Holy Relics: A Testament to the Sanctity of the Saints

By the grace of God, numerous churches are privileged to preserve and venerate the relics of the Saints. These sacred treasures have been obtained from revered holy sites, including the Holy Land (Jerusalem), Mount Athos, Greece, Russia, and other regions, serving as a testament to the Church's enduring spiritual heritage. While many parishioners understand the profound significance of venerating relics within Orthodox piety, some may be less familiar with this essential practice.

Saint Justin Popović,[16] Archimandrite of the Ćelije Monastery in Serbia, who reposed in 1979, writes in his article, *The Place of Holy Relics in the Orthodox Church*: "Holy Revelation indicates that by God's immeasurable love for mankind, the Holy Spirit abides through His grace not only in the bodies of the Saints but also in

---

[16] **Saint Justin Popović**: A 20th-century Serbian Orthodox theologian, ascetic, and hieromonk (1894–1979), renowned for his profound spiritual writings and contributions to Orthodox theology. As Archimandrite of Ćelije Monastery, he was a staunch defender of Orthodox tradition and an outspoken critic of secularism and ecumenism. His magnum opus, The Lives of the Saints, is a monumental hagiographic work that spans 12 volumes. Saint Justin's teachings emphasize the sanctity of human life, the centrality of Christ in all aspects of existence, and the transformative power of divine grace. He was glorified as a saint by the Serbian Orthodox Church in 2010, and his feast day is celebrated on June 1st / June 14th.

their clothing." This profound truth is evidenced by several examples in Holy Scripture.

In 2 Kings 13:8, we read how the Prophet Elijah "took his mantle, rolled it up, and struck the water" of the Jordan River. The waters parted, allowing him and his disciple Elisha to cross over. Later, in verse 14, after Elijah "was taken up into heaven by a whirlwind," Elisha took up the same mantle, struck the water, and it parted once again, enabling him to cross over (v. 14).

The healing power of holy objects is also evident in the New Testament. All four Gospels recount the story of the woman who suffered from a flow of blood for twelve years. In her desperation, she sought out Jesus, and amidst the crowd, she "came from behind and touched the hem of His garment. For she said to herself, 'If only I may touch His garment, I shall be made well.'" Jesus turned to her and said, "Be of good cheer, daughter; your faith has made you well." From that very moment, the woman was healed (Matthew 9:20–22). Mark and Luke add that Jesus, sensing power leaving Him, asked, "Who touched Me?" (Mark 5:30; Luke 8:45–46). Notably, the woman's healing came through her faith and her touching of His garment—not through direct physical contact with His body.

In Acts 19:11–12, we are told that "God worked unusual miracles by the hands of Paul, so that even handkerchiefs or aprons were brought from his body to the sick, and the diseases left them, and the evil spirits went out of them." Similarly, in Acts 5:15, we find the extraordinary account of people in Jerusalem bringing the sick into the streets, laying them on beds and couches, hoping "that at least the shadow of Peter passing by might fall on some of them."

A shadow, being intangible, underscores the miraculous power of faith. As St. Justin Popovich explains, "By His inexpressible love for man, the Divine Lord allows the servants of His Divinity to work miracles not only through their bodies and clothing but even with the shadow of their bodies, as demonstrated in this occurrence with the holy Apostle Peter."

The human body is a profound mystery, a fusion of the physical and spiritual, created by God and imbued with divine purpose. Matter, especially the human body, was not only created by God but is also inherently oriented toward God. The Incarnation of Christ—the Word made flesh (John 1:14)—reveals the sanctification of matter. Through His incarnation, Christ demonstrated that both soul and body are created for God, and through Him, both are called to eternal glory. In Christ's Body, all creation embarks on a path of deification, sanctification, and resurrection.

The Church, as the Body of Christ, plays a central role in this divine work. Through the Church, the human body is sanctified by the Holy Spirit, becoming a temple of God. The Saints, who have lived lives of grace-filled holiness, reflect this sanctification not only in their souls but in their bodies as well. Their bodies, which have become vessels of the Holy Spirit, continue to radiate divine grace even after death.

The holiness of the Saints extends beyond their souls to their very bodies. Through their ascetic lives, they have filled both soul and body with the grace of the Holy Spirit. Therefore, the veneration of holy relics—an integral part of Orthodox tradition—is a natural extension of the Church's reverence for the Saints. When we venerate relics, we are honoring the entire person of the Saint, whose body and soul have been united in holiness. As the Apostle Paul reminds us, "Your bodies are temples of the Holy Spirit" (1 Corinthians 6:19), and thus, these relics are worthy of veneration as temples of God.

Throughout history, the Church has witnessed numerous miracles through the relics of the Saints, affirming their sanctity. By God's will, miracles of healing, protection, and spiritual comfort continue to be performed through these relics. As St. John Chrysostom once observed, the relics of Saints bring grace and blessings to all who approach them with faith.

The veneration of holy relics has its roots in Divine Revelation. In the Old Testament, we see how God worked miracles through the relics of His servants. For example, a dead man was resurrected when his body touched the bones of the Prophet Elisha (2 Kings 13:21). The New Testament elevates the human body to even greater heights. Through Christ's resurrection, the body is destined for eternal life, and this promise is extended to all humanity. The Apostles, too, witnessed the miraculous power of relics. The handkerchiefs of St. Paul healed the sick (Acts 19:12), and the shadow of St. Peter cured the afflicted (Acts 5:15-16).

The Church continues this tradition, preserving and venerating the relics of the Saints as vessels of God's grace. As St. Augustine teaches, the miracles performed through relics are a testament to the resurrection and the life to come. These miracles not only reveal God's power but also affirm the faith of the Saints, who bore witness to the truth of Christ's resurrection.

In the Orthodox understanding, the veneration of relics is not simply a matter of tradition; it is deeply connected to the mystery of the Incarnation. The body, sanctified by Christ's resurrection, is destined for eternal life, and the relics of the Saints serve as a reminder of this divine calling. The relics, often myrrh-streaming,[17] manifest the sweet fragrance of holiness, symbolizing the Christian's transformation into "a sweet-savor of Christ unto God" (2 Corinthians 2:15). The miracles associated with relics are not mere signs; they are tangible expressions of God's grace working through His Saints.

From the earliest days of the Church, Christians have revered the relics of martyrs and Saints, building churches upon their graves and incorporating relics into the celebration of the Divine Liturgy. This practice reflects the deep connection between the holiness of the Saints and the life of the Church. As the Seventh Ecumenical Council decreed, the relics of the Saints are a source of salvation-bearing grace, and their veneration is a sacred tradition passed down through the ages.

Holy relics are a living witness to the transformative power of God's grace. They remind us that the human body, through union with Christ, is destined for eternal glory. As temples of the Holy Spirit, the bodies of the Saints continue to work miracles, drawing us closer to the divine life. Through the veneration of relics, we

---

[17] **Myrrh-streaming**: A miraculous phenomenon in Orthodox Christianity where icons, relics, or the bodies of saints exude fragrant oil, known as myrrh. This myrrh is considered a sign of divine grace and presence, often associated with healing, blessing, and spiritual renewal. The myrrh-streaming serves as a tangible witness to the sanctity of the individual or object and is regarded as a gift of God to the faithful, inspiring devotion and strengthening faith. Notable examples include the Hawaiian Myrrh-Streaming Iveron Icon of the Mother of God and the relics of various saints.

honor the work of God in His Saints and participate in the same grace that sanctified their lives.

In this way, the mystery of holy relics lies at the heart of the Church's understanding of salvation. By venerating the relics of the Saints, we recognize that both body and soul are sanctified in Christ, and through the Church, we too are called to share in this holiness. As St. John Damascene reminds us, the relics of the Saints are fountains of salvation, pouring forth God's blessings upon all who approach them with faith. Let us, therefore, approach these holy relics with reverence and gratitude, mindful of the divine grace that continues to work through them for the salvation of all.

The Candle: A Light of Faith and Devotion

One of the first actions many Orthodox Christians take upon entering a church is lighting a candle. This simple act, done almost instinctively, is deeply symbolic and carries a profound spiritual significance. It is difficult to imagine an Orthodox church without the warm glow of candles illuminating icons and filling the space with their gentle light.

Blessed Simeon of Thessalonica,[18] a 15th-century theologian on the Divine Liturgy, reflects on the meaning of this act. He teaches

---

[18] **St. Simeon of Thessalonica**: A 15th-century Orthodox archbishop, theologian, and liturgical scholar who served as the Archbishop of Thessalonica during a period of great ecclesiastical and political turmoil. Known for his profound writings on Orthodox liturgy and theology, his most notable work, On the Holy Liturgy, provides an in-depth commentary on the Divine Liturgy and other services of the Church, emphasizing their spiritual meaning and symbolism. Simeon defended Orthodox tradition against various heresies and sought to guide the faithful in understanding the mysteries of the faith. He reposed in 1429, and his feast day is commemorated on September 15th / September 28th.

that the purity of beeswax symbolizes the purity and chastity of the person offering the candle. In lighting a candle, we express repentance for our self-will and stubbornness, seeking to humble ourselves before God. The softness of the wax represents our readiness to obey God, while the flame signifies our transformation through the fire of His love, becoming new creatures in Christ.

A candle is not merely an offering of light; it is a visible expression of faith and devotion. It symbolizes our connection to the Divine light and the warmth of our love for God, the Theotokos, the angels, and the saints. However, it is important that this act is not reduced to a mechanical or formal ritual. Lighting a candle should be accompanied by heartfelt prayer, even a simple one spoken in our own words. The external act must be an expression of our internal faith.

Candles play an essential role in many church services. The newly baptized hold candles, as do couples during the sacrament of marriage. At funerals, candles burn around the departed, representing the light of Christ. During processions, the faithful protect their burning candles from the wind as they walk in reverence.

There are no strict rules regarding the number of candles one should light or where they should be placed. Each candle is a voluntary offering, a small sacrifice to God. Whether large or small, the grace and significance of the candle remain the same. The intention behind the offering, not its size, is what matters.

It is common for people to light candles before icons of Christ, the Mother of God, or the saints. Some light candles for the health of their loved ones, while others offer them for the repose of the souls of the departed. If all spaces on the candle stand are filled, one should avoid extinguishing another candle to make room. Instead, it is better to ask an attendant for assistance or patiently wait for an appropriate moment. It is also important not to be disheartened if your candle is extinguished at the end of the service—the offering has already been accepted by God.

Many superstitions surround the lighting of candles, such as the belief that a candle should only be lit with the right hand or that a candle going out is a sign of misfortune. These notions are without merit. The true meaning of lighting a candle is far deeper than any superstition.

While the burning candle is a beautiful and meaningful symbol, it is essential to remember that our spiritual life is not limited to this outward act. The candle represents our prayer and devotion, but it is the burning of the heart in love for God that is most pleasing to Him. We are not saved by symbols alone, but by the grace of God. The candle serves as a reminder of this grace, calling us to deeper prayer, repentance, and communion with Christ.

Behavior in Church

New parishioners often ask how they should behave during church services. This question is important because everything that takes place externally in the church is meant to reflect our internal spiritual state. It is essential to understand that our actions in the church, such as prostrations or making the sign of the Cross, are not mere rituals but expressions of our inner feelings. For example, a prostration is a sign of humility, and when we bow, our hearts should bow in humility as well. Without the inner disposition of humility, prostrations become an empty formality. Similarly, when we make the sign of the Cross, we express our faith in the crucified Lord. This outward gesture should unite with our thoughts and feelings toward the Cross of Christ, Whose sign we place upon ourselves. Otherwise, as some have described it, the act becomes mere "hand-waving" or, as was once said, "polishing buttons." The words of our prayers, too, should be filled with meaning, flowing from the heart. Otherwise, prayer is reduced to an empty gesture, devoid of any spiritual content.

In our spiritual lives, external expressions such as rituals and physical gestures are secondary to the inner state of the soul. The Gospels teach us that the spiritual aspect is far more important than the external. As Christ Himself said, "The Sabbath was made for man, and not man for the Sabbath" (Mark 2:27). He rebuked the scribes and Pharisees with these words from the Prophet Isaiah: "This people draweth nigh unto Me with their mouth, and honoureth Me with their lips, but their heart is far from Me" (Matthew 15:7-8). Our Lord's most pointed criticism was reserved for those whose external displays of piety were disconnected from their inner spiritual lives: "Woe unto you, scribes and Pharisees, hypocrites! For ye make clean the outside of the cup and of the platter, but within they are full of extortion and excess. Thou blind Pharisee, cleanse first that which is within the cup and platter, that the outside of them may be clean also" (Matthew 23:25-26). These rebukes remind us that outward religious actions without heartfelt participation amount to empty worship.

Punctuality and Respect in Church

Orthodox Christians should arrive at church on time and remain until the end of the service unless there is a compelling reason to leave early. Even in secular life, punctuality and respect for others are basic elements of good manners. How much more should this be the case in the house of God? Leaving early or arriving late disrupts not only our worship but also the prayerful atmosphere for others.

Women traditionally enter the church with their heads covered, following the ancient practice rooted in Scripture (1 Corinthians 11:5-6). This modest practice emphasizes reverence and humility before God. In addition, attire in church should always reflect the sanctity of the space. For women, this means avoiding clothing such as slacks or dresses with hemlines above the knee. These guidelines for modesty are not about fashion but about showing respect for the sacredness of the service and the community gathered to worship. We are called to present ourselves before God in a manner fitting the occasion, mindful of the Gospel's teaching: "Therefore, if thou bring thy gift to the altar, and there rememberest that thy brother hath ought against thee; leave there thy gift before the altar, and go thy way; first be reconciled to thy brother, and then come and offer thy gift" (Matthew 5:23-24).

Fasting Before the Divine Liturgy

A time-honored Orthodox practice, especially in the Russian tradition, is to fast before the Divine Liturgy. This means not eating or drinking anything prior to receiving Holy Communion. The reverence for this practice is seen in the custom of consuming *antidoron* or *prosphora* only after the Liturgy on an empty stomach. In earlier times, if *prosphora* was brought to someone who had missed the Liturgy, they would refrain from consuming it if they had already eaten, instead saving it for the next morning to partake of on an empty stomach. This practice shows the deep respect and reverence with which Orthodox Christians approach the holy gifts. Consuming *prosphora* immediately after the Liturgy continues this practice, as it is typically done on an empty stomach.

The Necessity of Regular Attendance

Orthodox Christians are called to attend Sunday and festal services regularly. The Sixth Ecumenical Council (680–681) specifically admonishes both clergy and laity against habitual absence from services: "In case any Bishop, or Presbyter, or Deacon, or anyone else on the list of the Clergy, or any layman, without any graver necessity or any particular difficulty compelling him to absent himself from his own church for a very long time, fails to attend church on Sundays for three consecutive weeks, while living in the city, if he be a Cleric, let him be deposed from office; but if he be a layman, let him be removed from Communion" (Canon 80). This canon emphasizes the seriousness of participating in the communal worship of the Church, as this is essential to our spiritual growth and well-being.

Entering the Church and Acts of Reverence

Upon entering the church, it is customary to make the sign of the Cross three times, accompanied by a bow to the waist. After this, it is appropriate to venerate the festal icon, if present, and the other icons in the church. These acts of reverence are outward expressions of inner devotion. Additionally, one should bow in respect to fellow parishioners as a sign of Christian love and humility. Lighting candles before icons is a common practice, symbolizing prayers offered to God or the saints. However, it is important to be mindful not to disrupt the service, especially during the more solemn moments, such as the Small Entrance, the reading of the Gospel, the Cherubic Hymn, or the Eucharistic Canon.

Conduct During Services

During the Divine Liturgy and other services, it is essential to avoid unnecessary movement, especially during key moments such as the Small Entrance (when the Holy Gospels are brought out), the reading of the Scriptures, and the Eucharistic Canon (which begins with the exclamation "Let us stand well, let us stand with fear [of God]"). Movement is particularly discouraged when someone is reading from the center of the church, such as during the Six Psalms, as the text of Matins and the Typikon clearly indicate. Additionally, no movement should occur when the Royal Doors are open, symbolizing the direct connection between the altar and the faithful, or when clergy are performing a liturgical action in the center of the church. These practices ensure that the congregation remains attentive and respectful during the holiest parts of the service, preserving the solemnity of worship.

It is also important to offer *prosphora* for the health and repose of loved ones before the public part of the Liturgy begins, preferably during the Proskomedia (the preparation of the bread and wine). Offering *prosphora* just before the Cherubic Hymn or during the Great Entrance causes unnecessary delays in the service, as the priest must interrupt the Liturgy to complete the Proskomedia.

Men and Women's Placement in the Church

In traditional Orthodox practice, men and women stand on opposite sides of the church during services. Men stand on the right side, while women stand on the left, reflecting the placement of the icons of Christ and the Mother of God on the iconostasis. This custom promotes a sense of order and reverence within the church. Standing during services is an expression of respect and attentiveness. However, those who are sick, elderly, or caring for young children may sit if needed, without guilt or shame, as the Church accommodates individual circumstances with compassion.

The Sacred Atmosphere of the Church

The church is where the bloodless Sacrifice of Christ is offered, and it is where the angels and saints invisibly serve alongside us. As such, the church is no place for idle conversation or distractions. This is a basic principle of reverence. Nonetheless, it must be emphasized that talking during the service disrupts the atmosphere of prayer and disturbs others who are trying to focus on the divine words or prepare for confession. Not only does conversation disrupt the service, but it is also inappropriate for people to stand casually with their hands in their pockets or walk about unnecessarily. Parents should also ensure that children behave respectfully and are not consuming food or chewing gum during services.

Kissing Icons and Prostrations

When venerating icons, it is important to follow the established tradition. For icons of Christ, we kiss His feet. For icons of the

Theotokos or the saints, we kiss their hands. When venerating icons such as the Savior Not-Made-By-Hands or the Head of St. John the Baptist, we kiss the hair. These acts of veneration are more than simple gestures—they are expressions of love and reverence for Christ, His Mother, and His saints.

Prostrations, too, are an important part of Orthodox worship, especially during certain times in the Liturgy. Before performing a prostration, the heart and mind must be directed toward God. The external gesture is meaningless without the inner disposition. Prostrations are made when venerating the Cross, icons, the Gospel, or holy relics. The proper order is to make two small prostrations, kiss the holy object, and then make an additional small prostration. This reflects the reverence and humility required in approaching the sacred.

During the Great Entrance in the Divine Liturgy, we stand with bowed heads, for this moment symbolizes Christ's entry into Jerusalem before His Passion. We also bow our heads during the reading of the Holy Gospel to help us concentrate on the words being proclaimed. Furthermore, when the priest calls out, "Bow your heads unto the Lord," we do so attentively, as these moments reflect personal prayers being offered on behalf of the entire congregation.

Full Prostrations and Their Significance

Full prostrations, where the head touches the ground, symbolize profound humility before God. According to the rules of the Holy Orthodox Church, full prostrations are not made on Sundays because the Lord's Day is a celebration of Christ's Resurrection, a "little Pascha." On this day, we celebrate Christ's victory over death and the reconciliation of humanity to God. Full prostrations are, however, appropriate on weekdays during the Liturgy.

The first full prostration in the Liturgy occurs after the Creed, when the priest says, "Let us give thanks unto the Lord!" At this point, the choir responds, "It is meet and right to worship the Father, Son, and Holy Spirit…" This is the moment when the priest offers a prayer of thanksgiving, acknowledging God's blessings, both known and unknown, and the peaceful sacrifice about to be offered. This act of thanksgiving is the heart of the Eucharist, a term derived from the Greek word meaning "thanksgiving." All the faithful make a full prostration at this point to express their gratitude to God for their lives and for His many blessings.

The second full prostration occurs during the epiclesis, the moment of the Divine Liturgy when the priest invokes the Holy Spirit to consecrate the bread and wine into the Body and Blood of Christ. This transformation is at the heart of the Eucharistic mystery, and it is when the priest prays, "changing them by Thy Holy Spirit," that the faithful make a full prostration. This act signifies our profound reverence and awe in the presence of the Holy Mysteries, as Christ Himself becomes present in the Holy Gifts. At this sacred moment, the words "Amen, Amen, Amen!" resound, affirming the transformation and expressing the congregation's acknowledgment of the profound mystery before them.

A third full prostration is made in honor of the Mother of God. After the consecration of the Holy Gifts, the priest offers prayers of intercession, particularly calling to mind the Theotokos:

"Especially for our Most holy, Most pure, Most blessed, Most glorious Lady Theotokos and Ever-Virgin Mary." At this point, the choir sings "It is truly meet to bless thee, O Theotokos..." This prostration shows our veneration for the Mother of God, who played an integral role in the Incarnation, through which our salvation was accomplished. The faithful bow in recognition of her as "more honorable than the Cherubim and more glorious beyond compare than the Seraphim," offering a prostration of deep respect for her essential place in salvation history.

The fourth full prostration occurs during the singing of the Lord's Prayer, the *Our Father*, which Christ Himself gave to us (Matthew 6:9-13). As we pray, "Give us this day our daily bread," we are not only asking for ordinary sustenance but also for the Eucharistic Bread, the Body of Christ. At this moment, we bow deeply, expressing our prayer that God will grant us His divine Bread "this day" for the healing of both our soul and body. The *Our Father* (Lord's Prayer) is the most profound prayer in the Church, and the prostration serves as a sign of our total reliance on God for all things, both physical and spiritual.

A fifth full prostration is made during the Great Entrance when the Holy Gifts are brought out for the communion of the faithful. As the priest or deacon announces, "With fear of God, with faith and love draw nigh!" we bow before the Holy Gifts, recognizing Christ's real presence in the Eucharist. According to Orthodox belief, the bread and wine have now become the Body and Blood of Christ, and we show our reverence by bowing as if before Christ Himself. This moment in the Liturgy underscores the solemnity and sacredness of Holy Communion, reminding us to approach with deep faith and love.

The sixth and final full prostration of the Liturgy is made after the singing of "We have seen the True Light…" At this point, the priest silently prays: "Be Thou exalted above the heavens, O God, and Thy glory above all the earth!" This marks the final appearance of the Holy Gifts to the people before they are returned to the altar. It is a symbolic reenactment of Christ's Ascension into heaven, as described in the Gospel of Luke: "And they worshipped Him, and returned to Jerusalem with great joy" (Luke 24:52). The faithful bow in reverence, just as the Apostles did, acknowledging Christ's return to the Father. However, those who have received Holy Communion do not perform this final prostration, as they now carry Christ within them, having partaken of His Body and Blood.

The Sacredness of Communal Prayer

The Divine Liturgy is not a private prayer, but a communal act of worship that unites the clergy, the laity, and the heavenly hosts in offering praise and thanksgiving to God. The clergy and the laity together form the visible, earthly Church, while the icons around us remind us of the invisible Church—the saints, the Theotokos, and Christ Himself, who is mystically present in the altar. The iconostasis, with its depiction of Christ enthroned on the right side of the Royal Doors and the Theotokos on the left, reflects this heavenly reality, and we participate in this heavenly worship each time we attend the Liturgy.

In this context, the church is no ordinary building. It is the House of God, where the bloodless Sacrifice of Christ is offered, and the Powers of Heaven serve invisibly alongside us. As such, a particularly prayerful atmosphere should always prevail in the church. Every member of the congregation shares the responsibility of maintaining this sacred atmosphere, from the clergy to the laity. Idle conversation during services not only disrupts the peace of the church but also disturbs those who are trying to focus on the divine words and prepare their souls for confession or Holy Communion. It is not uncommon to witness some people, especially younger parishioners, standing casually with their hands in their pockets or walking aimlessly across the church during important moments in the Liturgy. Such behavior is inappropriate, as it detracts from the reverence that should characterize our worship.

Parents, too, have a special role in teaching their children how to behave respectfully in church. This includes ensuring that children do not chew gum, run around, or consume food during services. For instance, giving a young child an entire *prosphora* to hold often results in crumbs being dropped on the floor, where they may be trampled upon. Parents should instead give their children small pieces of *prosphora* at a time, so that the sacred bread is treated with the appropriate care. It is through these small, yet significant, practices that we instill a sense of reverence in the younger generation.

Guidelines for Proper Church Etiquette

To preserve the sacredness of the church and ensure that services proceed smoothly, certain guidelines should be observed:

- **Arriving on Time**: One should make every effort to arrive at the beginning of the divine service and remain until the end. Leaving early or arriving late disrupts the service and the prayer of others.

- **Entering the Church**: Upon entering, make the sign of the Cross and bow three times, showing reverence toward the altar. Avoid lingering at the entrance, as this may block others from entering.

- **Avoiding Transactions**: Conduct any monetary transactions, such as paying membership dues or purchasing candles, either before or after the service, avoid doing this during the service itself.

- **Men and Women's Placement**: As mentioned, men traditionally stand on the right side of the church and women on the left.

- **No Conversations**: Conversations, whether before, during, or after the service, should be avoided within the sacred space of the church.

- **Modesty in Attire**: Appropriate dress is expected of all parishioners. Immodest clothing, such as short dresses (hemlines above the knee), sleeveless tops, or attire with exposed shoulders, is inappropriate. Likewise, men and boys over seven should not wear T-shirts with offensive slogans or shorts to church. The church is not a place for casual attire.

- **Movement During the Liturgy**: Walking around or venerating icons during key moments of the service—such as the reading of the Gospel, the Cherubic Hymn, the Eucharistic Canon, or the Lord's Prayer—should be avoided.

The Importance of Sacred Space

During the Divine Services, certain moments are particularly sacred, and thus, movement or distraction should be avoided. These include:

- **At Vespers**: During the entrance of the priest or deacon with the censer, and during the reading of the Six Psalms, movement should be minimal.

- **At Matins**: During the reading of the Holy Gospel and the singing of the Great Doxology, attention and reverence should be at their highest.

- **At the Divine Liturgy**: The Little Entrance (with the Gospel), the Great Entrance (with the Chalice), the reading of the Epistles and Gospel, and the singing of the Cherubic Hymn are moments when stillness and prayer are most appropriate.

- **The Eucharistic Canon**: From the exclamation "The doors! The doors! In wisdom, let us attend!" through the singing of "It is truly meet..." is the heart of the Liturgy, and the faithful should stand with their full attention on the divine mystery unfolding before them.

- **The Lord's Prayer**: As we collectively recite the *Our Father*, we focus our prayers not just on our daily sustenance, but on the Eucharistic Bread, which gives life to our souls and bodies.

Worship in the Orthodox Church involves the whole person—body, mind, and soul. The physical movements of bowing, making the sign of the Cross, and performing prostrations are integral parts of our participation in the Liturgy, but they only carry meaning if they are united with our inner spiritual life. External actions without internal devotion are empty, and the Church emphasizes the importance of aligning our hearts with our physical expressions of prayer.

In the church, we stand in the presence of Christ, the Theotokos, and the saints, surrounded by the icons that remind us of the invisible Church. The Liturgy brings us into communion with Heaven, and we must conduct ourselves with the utmost reverence and attentiveness. By observing the guidelines of the Church and participating fully—both inwardly and outwardly—in the divine services, we offer true worship to God and grow in our spiritual lives.

On Venerating the Holy Gospels, the Cross, Holy Relics, and Icons

Venerating sacred objects such as the Holy Gospels, the Cross, relics of saints, and holy icons is a deeply revered practice in Orthodox Christianity. When approaching these holy items, it is important to do so with reverence and humility, maintaining order and avoiding any rush or crowding. The act of veneration involves more than a mere physical gesture; it is an expression of our faith and love for Christ, His saints, and the holy things that represent His presence among us.

When approaching to venerate, it is customary to make two prostrations before and one prostration after kissing the holy item. The type of prostration depends on the day and the liturgical rules governing that particular service. On regular weekdays, full prostrations are appropriate. These involve kneeling and touching one's forehead to the ground, symbolizing deep humility and submission before God. On Sundays and feast days, when the joy of the Resurrection is celebrated, smaller prostrations (deep bows where the hand touches the ground) are made instead, to reflect the more celebratory nature of the day.

Prayers When Venerating Icons and the Cross

When venerating an icon of the Savior, it is fitting to accompany the act with the recitation of the *Jesus Prayer*: "**Lord Jesus Christ, Son of God, have mercy upon me, a sinner.**" This prayer is simple yet profound, offering a moment of repentance and a direct appeal for Christ's mercy. Alternatively, one may say the prayer: "***I have sinned immeasurably, O Savior, have mercy upon me***," recognizing our sins and asking for divine forgiveness.

In front of an icon of the Most-Holy Theotokos, the faithful may pray: "***O Most-Holy Theotokos, save us.***" This prayer is a heartfelt appeal to the Mother of God, asking for her intercession and protection. The Theotokos is highly revered in Orthodox tradition, and this simple prayer expresses trust in her maternal care for all believers.

When venerating the Honorable and Life-Giving Cross of Christ, we say the prayer: "***Before Thy Cross, we bow down, O Master, and Thy Holy Resurrection we glorify.***" This prayer, full of reverence and awe, acknowledges both the sacrifice of Christ on the Cross and His glorious Resurrection. After reciting this prayer, it is customary to follow it with a prostration, bowing down before the Cross as a sign of deep respect and gratitude for the salvation it represents.

Venerating the holy Gospels, Cross, relics, and icons is an essential part of Orthodox worship, connecting the faithful to the sacred mysteries and the presence of Christ and His saints. These acts of veneration are not mere traditions but profound expressions of love, reverence, and faith. Through proper veneration and accompanying prayers, we align our hearts and bodies in worship, drawing closer to God and the heavenly kingdom. In all things, we are called to approach with humility, attentiveness, and a prayerful heart, making these sacred gestures a true offering of devotion.

Sanctified Bread in the Orthodox Tradition

Bread holds a deeply significant place in both daily life and religious practice. It symbolizes the sustenance we need to live and the labor required to earn it, as God declared to Adam: "In the sweat of thy face shalt thou eat bread" (Genesis 3:19). In this, bread becomes not only a symbol of physical nourishment but also of the human struggle and toil that sustains life.

Yet, beyond its earthly symbolism, bread carries profound religious meaning in Christianity. The Lord Jesus Christ described Himself as the "bread of life" (John 6:51) and promised, "If any man eat of this bread, he shall live forever" (John 6:51). Bread, made from grains of wheat that are transformed into something greater, became the very element Christ chose for the Holy Eucharist. In the Mystery of the Eucharist, bread is transubstantiated into the Body of Christ. As recounted in the Gospels, "Jesus took bread, and blessed it, and brake it, and gave it to the disciples and said, 'Take, eat; this is My body'" (Matthew 26:26).

Bread also reflects the nature of the Church itself. Just as bread is made from many grains, so the Church is composed of many members, yet remains one unified Body. This symbolism of unity and spiritual nourishment is expressed through several forms of sanctified bread within the Orthodox Church, each with its own purpose and significance.

The Prosphoron: Offering Bread

The *prosphoron* (from the Greek word meaning "offering") is a central element in Orthodox liturgical practice. It is a round, yeast-raised bread made from wheat flour, mixed with holy water. Its name comes from the early Christian tradition where believers would bring bread from home to offer for the celebration of the Eucharist.

The prosphoron consists of two round parts, symbolizing the two natures of Christ—His divinity and humanity. A cross is stamped on the upper part, signifying Christ's sacrificial death. Sometimes, images of the Mother of God or saints are stamped on prosphora, linking these offerings to the wider communion of the Church.

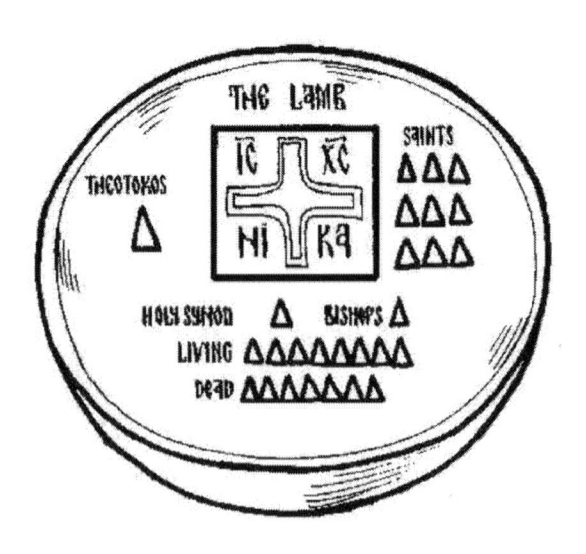

During the Divine Liturgy, a portion of the bread, called the Lamb, is taken from one of the prosphora in a rite of preparation known as the Proskomedia. This Lamb is the part of the bread that will be consecrated and become the Body of Christ. Other smaller prosphora are used in commemoration of both the living and the departed, members of both the Earthly and Heavenly Church. During the Liturgy, these particles of bread are placed into the Chalice with the Blood of Christ at the conclusion of the service, symbolizing the unity of the faithful with Christ through His sacrifice.

After the Liturgy, the remaining pieces of the prosphoron from which the Lamb was taken are called *antidoron,* meaning "instead of the Gifts." These pieces are distributed to those who have not communed, offering a sanctified blessing to all present, even if they did not receive the Holy Mysteries.

The Artos: Symbol of the Risen Christ

Artos is a special form of sanctified bread in the Orthodox Church, particularly associated with Pascha (Easter). Artos is a yeast-risen bread, symbolizing the Risen Christ. On the night of Pascha, this bread is blessed and placed on an *analogion* (a stand) before the Royal Doors of the Altar, where it remains throughout Bright Week. During this time, the *artos* is carried in the daily Paschal Processions, emphasizing the presence of the Resurrected Christ in the life of the Church.

On Bright Saturday, a special prayer is read, and the *artos* is broken into pieces and distributed to the faithful. This bread, linked to the joy of the Resurrection, is seen in pious tradition as a source of spiritual strength. In some folk customs, *artos* and Holy Water blessed at Theophany are given to those nearing death, especially when they cannot receive Holy Communion, as a final blessing and comfort.

Antidoron: Bread for the Faithful

Another important form of sanctified bread is *antidoron*. As mentioned earlier, this bread is distributed at the end of the Liturgy to those who did not receive Communion. Though it is not the Eucharist, it is sanctified and should be consumed with reverence. The practice of receiving *antidoron* connects the faithful to the sacramental life of the Church, even when they are not physically partaking in the Body and Blood of Christ. It is a reminder of the blessings of Christ's sacrifice, and those who partake should do so on an empty stomach and with a prayerful heart.

Orthodox tradition calls for *artos, prosphora,* and *antidoron* to be eaten on an empty stomach, a practice that emphasizes the sacred nature of these breads. They must also be stored separately from other food in a clean, dedicated container, as a sign of their sanctity. Many faithful divide the *artos* into small pieces and consume it gradually throughout the year, from Pascha to Pascha, as a constant reminder of Christ's Resurrection and the life He brings.

Sanctified Bread During Vigil

In addition to the use of sanctified bread during the Divine Liturgy, the Orthodox Church also distributes blessed bread during Vigils on the eves of great feasts. Historically, evening services were lengthy, and bread was given to the faithful to help them maintain their strength throughout the night. Although services today are typically shorter, this tradition has been retained as a way of connecting modern worship with the practices of the early Church.

Church Commemoration Lists: Guidelines and Importance

Submitting commemoration lists for prayer during the Divine Liturgy is a profound and cherished practice in the Orthodox Church. These lists allow the faithful to present the names of loved ones, both living and departed, before the altar, where they are remembered in the prayers of the Church. To ensure that these names are read attentively and with the reverence they deserve, it is important to follow certain guidelines.

Timing of Submission

For your commemoration lists to be properly included in the prayers, it is essential to submit them before the beginning of the Divine Liturgy. Ideally, you should offer your lists either the evening before or early in the morning, before the service starts. This allows the clergy sufficient time to prepare and include the names in the Proskomedia, the service of preparation before the Liturgy, where particles are taken from the *prosphora* for each name.

Writing with a Prayerful Heart

As you write down the names for commemoration, do so with a clean heart and a sincere intention. Remember those you are writing down, and offer them your heartfelt prayers, wishing them good and spiritual well-being. This act of writing is itself a form of prayer, as you bring to mind each person and present them before God with love and humility.

Order and Format of Names

When listing names for commemoration, it is important to follow the proper order and format:

1. **Clergy First**: Always list the names of bishops and priests first, including their ranks (e.g., "for the health of Bishop Tikhon, Abbot Tikhon, Priest Yaroslav"). After clergy, list your own name and then the names of your relatives and close acquaintances.

2. **Living and Reposed**: Separate the lists into those for the living ("for the salvation of") and those for the reposed ("for the repose of"). This distinction is crucial for the prayers offered at the altar.

3. **Legibility and Brevity**: Write the names clearly and legibly, ensuring that each name is easily readable. Limit the list to no more than 10 names per page to allow the clergy to read each name carefully and prayerfully.

4. **Language and Case**: If you are writing in Russian, make sure to use the genitive case for names. This is the proper grammatical form used in Church Slavonic prayers.

5. **Full First Names**: Always use the full form of the name, even when commemorating a child (e.g., use "Sergei" instead of "Seryozha"). This practice aligns with the tradition of using the saint's name in its full, formal version.

6. **Church Spelling of Names**: Be aware of the traditional church spellings for saints' names (e.g., "Ekaterina" instead of "Katya"; "Vladimir" instead of "Vova"; "Nicholas" instead of "Kolya").

Specific Considerations

- **Children's Ages**: When commemorating children, indicate their age category. A child under seven years is referred to as an "infant," while a child from seven to eighteen years is referred to as a "youth."

- **Avoid Surnames and Titles**: Do not include surnames, patronymics, titles, or professions in the list. Focus only on the first names, as these are what are commemorated during the prayers.

- **Appropriate Descriptors**: It is permissible to include specific conditions or statuses such as "warrior," "monk," "nun," "ill," "traveling," or "imprisoned." However, avoid using terms like "erring," "suffering," "embittered," "studying," "grieving," "virgin," "widow," or "pregnant," as these are not typically used in liturgical commemorations.

- **Commemorating the Reposed**: For those who have recently departed this life, use the term "newly-departed" if they have reposed within the past 40 days. For others, "ever memorable."

Offering Commemoration Lists

Commemoration lists can be offered for different services:

1. **Proskomedia**: During the Proskomedia, which is the first part of the Liturgy, particles are taken from *prosphoras* for each name listed. These particles are later placed into the

Chalice containing the Blood of Christ during the Liturgy, as a prayer for the remission of sins of those commemorated is read.

2. **Moleben and Panikhida**: Commemoration lists can also be offered for Moleben (services of supplication) and Panikhida (memorial services) that are served after the Liturgy. If you wish to have names commemorated during these services, submit separate lists specifically for this purpose.

By following these guidelines, you help ensure that the names you submit for commemoration are treated with the care and attention they deserve. This practice of submitting names is not just a ritual but an act of love and faith, connecting those we pray for to the grace of the Liturgy. In doing so, we participate in the communal life of the Church, offering up our loved ones to God's mercy and remembering them in the most sacred moments of worship.

A CHRISTIAN HOME

Saint John Chrysostom offers a profound example of the harmonious Christian household, grounded in Biblical models that continue to inspire believers today. He points to the example of Abraham and Sarah, drawing from the Old Testament to illustrate how a home can reflect unity, piety, and spiritual wholeness. Abraham, the father of faith, and Sarah, his devoted wife, embodied the principles of a household where all members, from family to servants, operated in unison, fulfilling the divine purpose. Chrysostom emphasizes this harmonious unity: *"Consider Abraham and Sarah, and Isaac and the three hundred and eighteen born in his house..."* (Genesis 14:14). Their household was not only prosperous materially but also spiritually, marked by deep respect and mutual love.

Chrysostom highlights how Sarah reverenced her husband, calling him "lord" (Genesis 18:12), which was an expression of her respect for Abraham's spiritual leadership. At the same time, Abraham's love for Sarah was evident in his deference to her in matters of family life, showing that a godly home is one where mutual respect and love flourish. Their servants, too, were committed to the household's mission, so much so that one servant was trusted with arranging the marriage of Abraham's son, Isaac (Genesis 24:1-67). This holistic harmony extended beyond familial relations to everyone under their roof, demonstrating that a family grounded in faith can achieve great things together. Just as a well-organized army or ship is fortified against attack, so a Christian household, united in faith, stands firm against spiritual adversity.

In his analogy, Chrysostom draws attention to the detrimental impact of even one unfaithful or disobedient member on the household. He cautions that the whole house can be "overthrown and broken up by one bad servant," illustrating the destructive power of discord. The underlying message is that every family member plays a critical role in maintaining the household's spiritual health and well-being.

The Christian Home: Simplicity and Spirituality

A Christian home, according to St. John Chrysostom, should be a place of sobriety and simplicity, reflecting the spiritual goals of its inhabitants. He emphasizes that the beauty of a home should not descend into opulence, warning, *"what is handsome [should not] degenerate into finery."* The home should reflect the family's commitment to spiritual growth rather than the accumulation of material wealth. In fact, Chrysostom goes further, suggesting that luxury and excess are not just unnecessary, but actively harmful to the soul. "Luxuries and money are worse than ordinary dust and dirt," he writes, underscoring that while ordinary dust sullies the physical environment, material excess corrupts the soul.

Simplicity in the Christian home frees its inhabitants from the anxieties that often accompany wealth and possessions. Chrysostom offers three key benefits of this simplicity: first, the wife will not grieve if household items are stolen or damaged, knowing that her true treasures are spiritual, not material. Second, the husband will not be burdened by the need to protect or accumulate more wealth, allowing him to focus on matters of eternal importance. Third, both husband and wife will avoid finding undue pleasure in material possessions, freeing their hearts to concern themselves with God and their spiritual duties.

This emphasis on simplicity is not only about aesthetics but is deeply tied to the spiritual atmosphere of the home. A house filled with material distractions makes it harder for its members to focus on spiritual pursuits. By keeping their home simple and unpretentious, Christians can cultivate an environment where spiritual matters take precedence over material concerns.

The Family Church: A Place of Worship and Salvation

St. John Chrysostom profoundly describes the Christian home as a family church, a sacred place where the family members can live out their faith on a daily basis. This concept is rooted in the idea that the home is the primary setting for learning and practicing the faith. It is within the home that children are raised to love and honor God, where parents model Christian behavior, and where daily acts of piety are encouraged. Chrysostom refers to the example of Aquila and Priscilla, who, as the Bible tells us, made their house a place of worship: "They had made their very house a church" (1 Corinthians 16:19).

However, Chrysostom is clear that the family church cannot function in isolation. It must remain a part of the broader parish community, drawing strength from its connection to the local church. The family church is not independent of the parish but serves as an extension of it. Chrysostom warns that if a family decides to sever its ties with the parish church, it risks losing the outpouring of God's grace that nourishes the household. Such a family church ceases to be a spiritual refuge, becoming a house without the spiritual blessings that flow from its connection to the wider Church.

The purpose of the family church is identical to that of Christian marriage: the pursuit of eternal salvation. To achieve this, the family must stay closely aligned with the parish church, drawing on the grace, strength, and guidance that it offers. A family that cuts itself off from the parish church will soon find its spiritual life dwindling, as it is no longer rooted in the divine truths that are protected and taught within the Church. No Christian life can be lived in isolation, and to separate oneself from the Church is to sever one's spiritual lifeline.

The Blessing of the Home and Family as a Church

The Orthodox Christian home is consecrated through the blessing of the home, a sacramental service performed by a priest. This blessing is typically conducted soon after moving into a new home, but it is also a regular occurrence, particularly during the season of Theophany, when the house is blessed with holy water that has been sanctified in the parish church. The blessing of the home helps to maintain the spiritual connection between the family church and the parish church, reinforcing the idea that the family is an integral part of the broader Body of Christ.

During the house blessing, the priest sprinkles holy water in every room of the house, praying for God's protection and sanctification of the dwelling. The icon corner is often the focus of this blessing, as it serves as the spiritual center of the home. This ritual is not merely symbolic but is believed to bring real spiritual benefits to the family, driving away any evil influences and filling the home with God's grace.

Families are also encouraged to invite the priest for periodic blessings, especially during major feasts or times of personal significance, such as after the birth of a child or before significant life events. These blessings help renew the family's commitment to live according to Christian principles and keep the household grounded in faith.

Spiritual Protection and the Power of Holy Objects

Orthodox Christianity holds that certain holy objects, such as holy water, blessed oil, and icons, provide spiritual protection and serve as tangible means of receiving God's grace. In times of illness or spiritual struggle, Orthodox families often make use of these blessed items to strengthen their faith and drive away any evil influences that may threaten the household.

Holy water is particularly significant and is often used to sprinkle the home, especially the icon corner, as a form of spiritual cleansing. Drinking holy water is a common practice, particularly in times of illness or temptation, reminding the faithful of their baptismal cleansing and their ongoing participation in the life of Christ. Blessed oil, often obtained from oil lamps burning before holy relics or miraculous icons, is also used for anointing family members, symbolizing the healing and merciful grace of God.

The spiritual warfare described in Scripture is a daily reality for Orthodox Christians, who view their home as a battleground for the soul. Through the use of these holy objects and the regular participation in prayer and sacramental life, the family seeks to shield itself from the attacks of the evil one and maintain a holy and peaceful household.

The Christian Home as a Place of Forgiveness

One of the most important aspects of the Orthodox Christian home is the practice of forgiveness. In a world filled with conflicts and misunderstandings, the family church is called to be a place where reconciliation and forgiveness are practiced regularly. St. John Chrysostom teaches that forgiveness is the cornerstone of the Christian life, and without it, no one can expect to receive God's mercy.

Forgiveness within the family is not just a matter of resolving conflicts but is seen as a spiritual exercise that draws the family closer to God. Orthodox families often practice asking for forgiveness from one another at the end of each day, particularly before going to bed. This humble practice ensures that anger, resentment, or bitterness do not take root in the heart, making way for the peace and unity that Christ desires for His followers.

In the lead-up to receiving the Holy Eucharist, forgiveness becomes even more essential. The Orthodox Church teaches that anyone approaching the Eucharist must first be reconciled with their brothers and sisters, in keeping with Christ's words: *"If you bring your gift to the altar and there remember that your brother has something against you, leave your gift there before the altar, and go your way. First, be reconciled to your brother, and then come and offer your gift"* (Matthew 5:23-24). This practice ensures that the family remains united in love and peace, a reflection of the broader unity of the Church.

Fasting and Asceticism in the Christian Home

Fasting is another fundamental aspect of Orthodox Christian life, deeply rooted in both the Old and New Testaments. The family church is called to observe the fasting periods of the Church, which include not only abstaining from certain foods but also fasting from sin and negative behaviors. As St. Basil the Great states, *"Fasting is not merely abstaining from food, but also from sinful behaviors. If you are fasting from food, ensure that your actions are in harmony with the fast."*

In the Christian household, fasting is observed as a family practice, with meals becoming simpler and the focus shifting to spiritual nourishment. Children are taught the value of fasting from a young age, not as a burden but as a way of drawing closer to God and cultivating self-discipline. Fasting periods are often accompanied by increased prayer, Scripture reading, and acts of charity, helping the family to focus on the spiritual rather than the material aspects of life.

The Family Church as the Path to Salvation

The Orthodox Christian family home is not just a physical dwelling but a family church, a sacred space where every aspect of life is oriented toward spiritual growth and salvation. Through the practice of daily prayer, fasting, the veneration of icons, and the use of holy objects, the family participates in the life of the Church and draws closer to God. The family church is intimately connected to the parish church, relying on the sacraments and the guidance of the priest to remain steadfast in the faith.

Ultimately, the purpose of the family church is the same as that of Christian marriage: the attainment of eternal salvation. By living according to the teachings of Christ and the Church, the family becomes a miniature version of the Church, reflecting the love, peace, and holiness of God in every aspect of life. As St. John Chrysostom reminds us, a Christian household that is united in faith and love becomes a fortress against the world's temptations, a place where Christ is present and the family is safeguarded by His grace.

Home Prayer Corner or Room

The desire for a richer, more structured prayer life is a common aspiration among Orthodox Christians, particularly as one seeks to deepen their relationship with God through regular daily prayers. A significant way to support this spiritual resolution is by creating a designated space in the home specifically for prayer. This sacred area, known as a prayer corner or "home altar," has long been a treasured tradition within the Orthodox faith.

At its simplest, a prayer corner may consist of a small shelf or table adorned with a few carefully chosen icons, set aside exclusively for the purpose of prayer. For some, this sacred space may encompass an entire wall, or in more devout households, an entire room is transformed into a chapel. Regardless of the size or complexity, the prayer corner's function remains the same: to provide a dedicated place where one can retreat from the distractions of daily life and enter into communion with God.

When establishing a prayer corner, it is essential to remember that quality, not quantity, defines its spiritual effectiveness. It is a common misconception to believe that the more icons one has, the more pious or holy the home becomes. In reality, a cluttered or disorganized collection of icons, religious prints, and calendars can sometimes detract from a person's spiritual focus. The beauty and power of the icons are diminished if they are treated as mere decorations or collectibles, rather than sacred windows to the divine, intended to facilitate deeper prayer and reflection.

While it is important to have icons in the home, they should be present in sufficient numbers and arranged thoughtfully. Historically, Orthodox families always had a dedicated space for icons, known as the "bright corner," "holy corner," or "God's place." Whether in rural villages or urban settings, the icons were placed in the most visible and accessible part of the home, creating a focal point for family prayer and devotion.

Icons are far more than mere religious artwork or family heirlooms. In Orthodox Christian theology, the icon is a sacred depiction that transcends ordinary reality. It serves as a tangible link between the believer and the divine, facilitating prayer and communion with God. The primary purpose of the icon is to inspire prayer and to serve as a gateway to the heavenly realm. As such, icons should not be treated as mere decorations or relics to be passed down through generations. Rather, they are holy objects that unite the family in communal prayer. This unity is essential, as communal prayer can only take place when those praying have forgiven one another and stand before the icon in a spirit of harmony.

Unfortunately, in modern times, the place once reserved for the family icon has often been supplanted by the television, a device that, in many ways, serves as a window into the chaotic and passion-driven world. The prominence of the television in the home has contributed to the decline of the tradition of common prayer and the concept of the family as the "little Church." As a result, many Orthodox Christians today are left wondering what role icons should play in their homes, how they should be arranged, and whether reproductions or old, dilapidated icons still hold spiritual value.

When deciding where to place icons in the home, it is preferable to position them on the eastern wall of the room, as the East holds theological significance in the Orthodox tradition. Throughout Scripture, the East is repeatedly associated with divine revelation and the coming of God's presence. For example, in the book of Genesis, we read that God planted a garden eastward in Eden (Genesis 2:8). Similarly, in the Gospel of Matthew, Christ's return is foretold to come "as the lightning comes out of the east" (Matthew 24:27). However, if the layout of your home does not allow for an eastern-facing icon corner, other walls, such as the southern, northern, or western sides, may be used.

It is important to keep icons separate from secular objects, such as decorative statuettes or unrelated wall hangings. Similarly, icons should not be placed alongside books that conflict with Christian teachings or next to images of popular culture figures, such as musicians or politicians. This juxtaposition diminishes the sacredness of the icons and places them on an equal footing with worldly idols, undermining the reverence they deserve.

To further enhance the beauty of the prayer corner, icons may be decorated with fresh flowers or framed with embroidered towels, a practice that dates back to ancient traditions. According to Church Tradition, Christ once wiped His face with a towel, leaving an imprint of His image, which was then sent to King Abgar of Edessa, who was miraculously healed. This holy relic became known as the "Image-Not-Made-By-Hands" and marked the beginning of a tradition where icons are often adorned with towels, particularly on significant feast days like the Feast of the Holy Trinity or Palm Sunday.

In terms of which icons should be included in the home, it is essential to have at least two: an icon of Christ and one of the Theotokos (Mother of God). These two icons are foundational to Orthodox spirituality, as they represent the Incarnation of Christ and the deification of humanity through the Mother of God. The most common icon of Christ for home prayer is that of the *Pantokrator*, a depiction of Christ as the Ruler of All. Alongside these, Orthodox Christians often venerate Saint Nicholas the Wonderworker, who holds a special place in Russian Orthodoxy and is beloved for his miracles and compassionate intercession. In Russian culture, there is a well-known saying: **Без Троицы дом не строится** (Bez Troitsy dom ne stroitsya), meaning, "Without the Trinity, a house cannot be built." This reflects the deeply ingrained spiritual belief in the importance of the Holy Trinity as a foundation for life. As a result, it is often recommended to include an icon of the Holy Trinity in the home, symbolizing divine presence and blessing.

For those with the space to include more icons, you may add additional representations of revered saints, prophets, and martyrs. Common choices include icons of St. George the Trophy-Bearer, St. Panteleimon the Healer,[19] the Holy Apostles Peter and

---

[19] **St. George the Trophy-Bearer:** A great martyr and military saint of the Orthodox Church, revered for his steadfast faith and courage under persecution.

Paul, and the Archangels Michael and Gabriel. Additionally, saints from one's specific tradition or diaspora, such as St. John of Kronstadt or St. Seraphim of Sarov[20] for those in the Russian Orthodox Church, can be included to personalize the iconography according to your heritage and spiritual devotions. A complete home iconostasis may also feature icons of the Holy Feasts, adding depth to the visual and spiritual significance of the prayer corner.

The selection and arrangement of icons are deeply personal matters and should ideally be guided by a spiritual advisor or family priest. When choosing icons, it is better to have a high-quality reproduction of a canonical icon than a poorly executed original. The iconographer bears the same level of responsibility

---

Born in the 3rd century in Cappadocia, St. George was a Roman soldier who openly confessed his Christian faith during the reign of Emperor Diocletian, resulting in his martyrdom. Known as the "Trophy-Bearer" for his spiritual victories over evil, St. George is celebrated as a patron of soldiers and defenders of the faith. His feast day is commemorated on April 23rd / May 6th.

St. Panteleimon the Healer: A 4th-century martyr and unmercenary healer, renowned for his compassion and miraculous healings. Born in Nicomedia, St. Panteleimon was a physician who dedicated his medical practice to serving the poor and suffering without charge. After converting to Christianity, he used his medical skills to glorify God, healing both physical and spiritual ailments. He was martyred during the reign of Emperor Maximian for refusing to renounce his faith. His feast day is commemorated on July 27th / August 9th.

[20] **St. Seraphim of Sarov:** A revered 18th–19th century Russian Orthodox monk, mystic, and wonderworker (1754–1833), renowned for his profound spiritual wisdom and humility. Born Prokhor Moshnin, he entered the Sarov Monastery at a young age, dedicating his life to prayer, asceticism, and solitude. St. Seraphim is especially known for his teaching on the acquisition of the Holy Spirit and his practice of greeting visitors with the joyful words, "Christ is Risen!" His encounter with Nicholas Motovilov, in which he explained the purpose of Christian life, remains a foundational text of Orthodox spirituality. Glorified as a saint in 1903, St. Seraphim is venerated for his miracles, healings, and his message of peace and joy in the Lord. His feast day is celebrated on January 2nd / January 15th.

for their work as the priest does when celebrating the Divine Liturgy. Therefore, if an icon's depiction is theologically questionable or aesthetically inappropriate, it is best to avoid purchasing it.

When arranging the icons, a sense of symmetry and order is crucial. Icons should be arranged in a way that reflects the hierarchy of the Church, with Christ and the Theotokos at the center. Locally venerated saints and other holy figures should not be placed above the icons of Christ, the Mother of God, or the Holy Trinity. In a classic iconostasis, the icon of Christ is placed to the right, and the Theotokos to the left.

Reverence for holy objects, such as icons, reflects our understanding of holiness as an attribute of God. Just as God is holy, so too are the saints and sacred objects that reflect His divine presence. Icons play a central role in the spiritual lives of Orthodox Christians, from the moment of baptism to the final prayers at the time of death. A proper reverence for icons should be instilled in children from an early age, teaching them to respect these holy images as representations of eternal realities.

It is preferable to have a well-made paper icon rather than a poorly painted one. A well-printed icon, even on paper, can effectively convey the beauty and spiritual significance intended, whereas a poorly painted icon may lack the dignity and reverence due to sacred imagery. While paper icons are a relatively recent development, it is indeed preferable to have a well-painted icon in the canonical style, as these traditionally crafted icons adhere closely to the sacred standards established by the Church. Paper icons do serve an important purpose, especially considering the expense of painted icons, making them more accessible to many faithful. However, it is unwise to be overly polemical about the quality or style of certain icons, as their true value lies in the faith and devotion they inspire.

For instance, the icon of the Mother of God, known as the "Milk-Giver," housed at St. Tikhon's House in San Francisco, may appear simple or even naive in its style. Yet, this icon was a profound source of spiritual strength and consolation for St. John Maximovitch of Shanghai and San Francisco,[21] who prayed before it fervently. Many miracles have been attributed to this icon, experienced by St. John himself and countless others.

If an icon becomes damaged or deteriorates over time, it should not be thrown away. Instead, it should be taken to the church to be burned, and the ashes buried in a sacred place, such as a cemetery or garden. Icons, even in their physical decay, continue to carry spiritual significance and should always be treated with respect.

The faces that gaze out from the icons represent eternity. As we stand before them in prayer, we are reminded of our connection to the divine and the call to repentance and spiritual

---

[21] **St. John Maximovitch of Shanghai and San Francisco:** A 20th-century Orthodox hierarch, wonderworker, and ascetic (1896–1966), renowned for his holiness, humility, and tireless pastoral care. Born in Imperial Russia, St. John served as bishop in Shanghai, where he cared for orphans, established churches, and protected his flock during times of great turmoil. Later, as Archbishop of San Francisco, he continued his missionary work, building the Holy Virgin Cathedral, caring for the poor, and performing countless miracles. Known for his strict asceticism and deep prayer life, St. John never slept in a bed, often praying throughout the night. He reposed in 1966 and was glorified as a saint in 1994 by the Russian Orthodox Church Outside of Russia (ROCOR). His incorrupt relics rest in San Francisco, and his feast day is celebrated on July 2nd / July 15th.

transformation. Through the intercession of the saints depicted in these sacred images, we are drawn closer to our Creator, constantly striving to perfect our souls and live in communion with God.

A Journey into the Heart of Orthodox Worship

Orthodox Christian worship invites believers into a sacred space where the temporal and eternal meet, a place of reverence, mystery, and profound communion with God. Every element of the Orthodox tradition—whether it be the unhurried rhythm of the Divine Liturgy, the harmonious flow of a cappella chants, or the veneration of icons and holy objects—serves to immerse the faithful in an experience of heaven on earth. The iconostasis, the sign of the cross, the kiss of peace, and the Eucharist all point to a deeper truth: that through Christ, the division between heaven and earth has been overcome, and we are invited to participate in the eternal worship of the Kingdom.

The structure, repetition, and beauty of Orthodox worship are not mere formalities but are designed to engage both the heart and mind, allowing the soul to rest in the presence of God. As time passes, these practices take root in the believer's life, forming a spiritual rhythm that extends beyond the walls of the church and into everyday life. The prayers, hymns, and sacred actions become second nature, carrying with them the timeless truths of the faith and drawing each worshipper closer to Christ and His Body, the Church.

In a world that often rushes from one moment to the next, the Orthodox Church calls us to slow down, to breathe, and to embrace the profound mystery of God's presence among us. Whether through the sacred music, the holy icons, or the transformative power of the Eucharist, Orthodox worship is an invitation to dwell in the presence of the divine and to be renewed by it. As we journey deeper into this sacred tradition, we come to realize that we are not just participants in an ancient ritual, but partakers in the eternal life and love of God.

CONCLUDING STATEMENT ON CHRISTIANITY AND ORTHODOXY

Archimandrite Sergius, a renowned theologian and spiritual father at the Russian Convent of the Holy Protection in Sofia, Bulgaria, has long been a significant figure in the preservation and defense of Orthodox Christian tradition. His refusal to accept the New Revised Calendar, or what is often referred to as the "Papal Calendar," resulted in his dismissal from his post as Assistant Professor at the Theological Academy in Sofia. Despite facing academic and institutional consequences, his unwavering commitment to Orthodox tradition earned him the respect and admiration of traditionalist believers in Bulgaria and beyond. He is rightly considered a confessor of the Orthodox Faith, standing firm in defense of the true teachings of Christ and the Apostolic Tradition.

In his essay written to commemorate the Sunday of Orthodoxy[22] in 1998, Archimandrite Sergius delves into the rich and multifaceted history of the Orthodox Church, examining how it has continuously safeguarded the true Christian faith through centuries of persecution, heresy, and internal dissent. He begins by reminding us of the earliest days of the Church, noting that

---

[22] **Sunday of Orthodoxy:** The first Sunday of Great Lent, commemorating the triumph of the Orthodox faith over iconoclasm and the restoration of the veneration of holy icons in 843. This feast marks the victory of the Church in affirming the Orthodox doctrine of the Incarnation, which upholds the legitimacy of depicting Christ, the Theotokos, and the saints in sacred images. Traditionally, a special procession with icons takes place, and the Synodikon of Orthodoxy is proclaimed, reaffirming the true faith. The Sunday of Orthodoxy serves as a reminder of the Church's unwavering commitment to the Apostolic faith and the victory of truth over heresy.

from the time of the Apostles, Christ's disciples were known as those who "call on the name of our Lord Jesus Christ" (1 Corinthians 1:2; Acts 9:14, 21). This identity as followers of Christ was not merely a label but a profound spiritual calling. Early Christians, such as the Holy Apostles, were persecuted precisely because they bore the name of Christ, and they rejoiced in their sufferings, knowing they were sharing in the sufferings of their Savior (Acts 5:41).

Archimandrite Sergius emphasizes that the name "Christian" itself—first given to the disciples in Antioch (Acts 11:26)—marked the beginning of Christianity as a distinct religious identity, separate from Judaism. This appellation was more than a term; it was a declaration of their commitment to follow Christ and uphold His teachings. The great Fathers of the Church, such as St. Cyril of Jerusalem and St. Athanasios the Great, affirmed this identity, reminding believers that through Christ, they were not only Christians by name but also in their manner of life and adherence to the truth.

The Defense Against Heresy: The Battle for Orthodoxy

As Archimandrite Sergius highlights, from the very beginnings of the Church, the early Christian faith faced opposition from various external forces. Many among the Jewish authorities and the pagan world struggled to accept Christ as the Messiah and sought to suppress His followers. Despite these trials, the Church, strengthened by divine grace, endured and flourished, bearing witness to the truth of the Gospel. However, perhaps more dangerous were the internal enemies—false teachers and heretics—who arose from within the Church itself. These individuals professed to be Christians but distorted the true teachings of Christ, leading others astray. St. Paul warned against these individuals, describing them as having "a form of godliness but denying its power" (2 Timothy 3:5). Likewise, St. John the Theologian referred to these false teachers as "antichrists" (1 John 2:18) and urged believers to avoid them, as they had abandoned the true faith (2 John 10-11).

Throughout the centuries, the Orthodox Church faced various heresies, from Arianism to Nestorianism, that threatened to corrupt the true teachings of Christ. Archimandrite Sergius explains that the Church Fathers, such as St. Justin the Philosopher and Clement of Alexandria, were steadfast in their defense of Orthodoxy, distinguishing true Christians from those who claimed the name but taught erroneous doctrines. St. Justin, in his *Dialogue with Trypho the Jew*, contrasts false Christians, who confess Christ but distort His teachings, with the true disciples of Christ who uphold the "pure doctrine" of the Apostles.

It was during this time of theological struggle that the term "Orthodox" came to be associated with the true faith. As Archimandrite Sergius explains, the word "orthodox" comes from the Greek words "orthos" (meaning "right" or "true") and "doxa" (meaning "opinion" or "glory"). The term signifies "right belief" or "true worship," and it became the defining characteristic of those who upheld the apostolic teachings against the distortions of heretics. St. Athanasios of Alexandria, often referred to as the "Father of Orthodoxy," defended the Orthodox faith against the Arian heresy and asserted that Orthodoxy alone preserved the true doctrine of Christ.

The Triumph of Orthodoxy

Archimandrite Sergius continues by explaining the pivotal role of the Ecumenical Councils in preserving the Orthodox faith. These councils, particularly the First Council of Nicaea in 325 AD, played a critical role in defining and defending Orthodox doctrine against heretical teachings. At Nicaea, the bishops of the Church, guided by the Holy Spirit, affirmed the divinity of Christ and condemned the teachings of Arius,[23] thus preserving the true doctrine of the Incarnation.

The Sunday of Orthodoxy, which commemorates the triumph of the Church over the Iconoclast heresy in the 9th century, is a testament to the Church's ongoing struggle to defend the true faith. The iconoclasts sought to remove the veneration of icons from Christian worship, but the Orthodox Church, guided by the Holy Fathers, upheld the veneration of icons as a legitimate and necessary expression of the Incarnation. As Archimandrite Sergius explains, the victory of the Church over the iconoclasts was not just a victory for the veneration of icons but a victory for the entirety of Orthodox doctrine, which had been under attack.

St. John of Damascus, one of the great defenders of icons, articulated the theological foundation for their veneration,

---

[23] **Arius:** A 4th-century presbyter of Alexandria (ca. 256–336) and the founder of Arianism, a Christological heresy that denied the full divinity of Christ. Arius taught that the Son of God was a created being, distinct from and subordinate to the Father, contradicting the Orthodox doctrine of the Holy Trinity. His teachings sparked a major theological crisis, leading to the First Ecumenical Council of Nicaea in 325, where Arianism was condemned, and the Nicene Creed was established to affirm Christ's co-eternal and consubstantial nature with the Father. Despite being exiled, Arius gained temporary imperial favor before his sudden death in 336. His legacy remains a significant example of heretical deviation from Apostolic teaching.

explaining that icons are not worshipped in themselves but are windows to the divine. The Seventh Ecumenical Council, held in Nicaea in 787 AD, affirmed this teaching and declared that the veneration of icons was an essential part of Orthodox worship. The Sunday of Orthodoxy, which is celebrated on the first Sunday of Great Lent, marks the Church's victory in preserving this tradition.

The Preservation of Orthodox Doctrine: A Call to Vigilance

Archimandrite Sergius concludes his essay with a call to vigilance. He warns against the dangers of ecumenism, which seeks to blur the distinctions between Orthodoxy and other forms of Christianity. He emphasizes that Orthodoxy is not simply one denomination among many but the true and unaltered expression of the Christian faith, as handed down from Christ and the Apostles. Any deviation from this truth is a distortion of the Gospel, and Orthodox Christians must remain steadfast in their defense of the faith. The Orthodox Church, as Archimandrite Sergius reminds us, has remained the "pillar and ground of the truth" (1 Timothy 3:15) throughout the centuries, faithfully preserving the teachings of Christ through the guidance of the Holy Spirit. This unbroken continuity of faith is what sets Orthodoxy apart from other Christian denominations, and it is the reason why the Church has been able to withstand the various heresies and schisms that have arisen throughout history.

Orthodoxy as the True Faith

In conclusion, Archimandrite Sergius's reflections on the Sunday of Orthodoxy serve as a powerful reminder of the importance of preserving the true faith. The Orthodox Church, through its unwavering commitment to the teachings of Christ and the

Apostles, has stood firm against the forces of heresy and division. The Feast of Orthodoxy is not merely a historical commemoration but a living reminder that the true faith—Orthodoxy—must be defended and upheld in every generation.

As Orthodox Christians, we are called to remain faithful to the teachings of the Holy Fathers and the decisions of the Ecumenical Councils and Synod, knowing that in doing so, we are preserving the true faith of Christ. Archimandrite Sergius's essay challenges us to remain vigilant in our defense of Orthodoxy, recognizing that the truth of the Gospel is singular and that any deviation from this truth leads to spiritual peril. In the words of St. Paul, "Stand firm in the faith" (1 Corinthians 16:13), knowing that the Orthodox Church is the one true Church of Christ, entrusted with the fullness of His teachings and the grace of the Holy Spirit.

"Orthodox Christians must steadfastly remain in Orthodoxy, preserve oneness of mind with one another and unhypocritical love, guard purity of soul and body, reject evil and unclean intentions, temperately partake of food and drink, and above all adorn themselves with humility, not neglect hospitality, refrain from conflicts and not give honor and glory in anything to earthly life, but instead await a reward from God: the enjoyment of heavenly goods."

- St. Sergius of Radonezh

REFERENCES & SOURCES

A Defence of the Christian Religion, page 230, Bath, 1822. See W.E. Gladstone, *Vaticanism* page 48, 1875.

A Guide to Orthodox Life (Etna, CA: Center for Traditionalist Orthodox Studies, 1996), pp. 90-96.

Archbishop Seraphim (Sobolev), *The Distortion of Orthodox Truth in Russian Theological Thought* (Sofia, 1943), p. 213 [in Russian].

Brianchaninov, Bishop Ignatius, "On Reading the Gospel," *Orthodox Life,* July-August 1967, No. 4 (106), p. 9.

Brown, Raphael, *The Little Flowers of St. Francis.* Image Books, Garden City, N.Y., 1958, p 60.

Bulter, *First Vatican Council,* page 477.

Cavarnos, Constantine, *Byzantine Sacred Art,* Belmont, MA, 1983.

Cavarnos, Constantine. Byzantine Sacred Art. (Selections from the writings of Fotis Kontoglou.) New York: Vantage Press, 1957.

Collected Letters of Bishop Theophan, 2nd part, Letter 261, p 103.

Creation and Redemption, Vol. III of the *Collected Works of Georges Florovsky* (Belmont, MA: Nordland Publishing Co.), 1976, pp. 201.208. Bishop Michael, *Commentary on the Epistles,* Vol. I (Kiev, 1897), p. 279 [in Russian].

Cyril Mango, *The Homilies of Photius,* p. 294. Cf. St. Basil: "What the spoken account presents through the sense of hearing, the painting silently shows by representations" (*P.G.*, Vol. 94, col. 1401a).

Dumas, G., "La Stigmatisation chez les mystiques cretiens," *Revue des deux Mondes*, 1 May 1907; in Guerier, pp 315-317.

Essay on the Catholic Claims, page 300, Bishop J.W. Doyle, 1826.

Father Alexander. "Orthodox Catechism: Catechism of the Eastern Orthodox Church." Missionary Leaflet E2b, Holy Trinity Orthodox Mission. Editor: Bishop Alexander (Mileant). 466 Foothill Blvd, Box 397, La Canada, CA 91011. https://www.fatheralexander.org/booklets/english/catechism_ext.htm.

Florovsky, Georges, *Collected Works.* vol. 1, *Bible, Church, Tradition.* Belmont, MA: Nordland, 1972-79. This little gem is under 100 pages and a superb treatment of the Eastern Orthodox perspective on these issues.

Guerier, V., *Francis*, pp 312-313.

Holy Transfiguration Monastery, "Directions for Using the Wick Float," (Brookline, Mass.; n. d.).

Holy Transfiguration Orthodox Church. "Library: Christian Teachings." Holy Transfiguration Orthodox Church, http://www.holy-transfiguration.org/library_en/ct.html.

How the Pope Became Infallible, Pius IX and the Politics of Persuasion, page 107, August Bernhard Hasler, Translated by Peter Heinegg, Doubleday and Co. Inc., Garden City, New York, 1981.

Hyperconsciousness, On Mental Passions, 2nd ed., pp 65-74.

Idem, Orthodox Iconography, Belmont, MA, 1977.

Kadloubovsky, E. and Palmer, G., *Early Fathers from the Philokalia,* "St Isaac of Syria, Directions on Spiritual Training," Faber and Faber, London, 1959. (hereafter referred to as *Early Fathers*).

Kalokyris, Constantine D., *The Essence of Orthodox Iconography,* Brookline, MA, 1971.

Khrapovitsky, Antony, *Confession: A Series of Lectures on the Mystery of Repentance.* Holy Trinity Monastery Press, Jordanville, N.Y., 1975.

Khrapovitsky, op. cit., p. 45.

Ladner, Gebhart B., "The Concept of the Image in the Greek Fathers and the Byzantine Iconoclastic Controversy." In *Dumbarton Oaks Papers,* No. 7 (1953).

Lives of Saints, Book 11, pp 119-120.

Lossky, Vladimir, *The Mystical Theology of the Eastern Church,* London, 1973.

Lossky, Vladimir, *The Mystical Theology of the Eastern Orthodox Church.* London, 1973.

M. J. Congar, O.P., *Chretiens desunis. Principes d'un 'oecumenisme' catholique,* Paris, 1937, p. 15. English translation by M. A. Bousfield, *Divided Christendom,* London, 1939, p. 13

Macarius, op. cit., p. 65.

Mansi, *Amplissima Collectio Conciliorum* (ParisLeipzig, 1901), Vol. VI, Col. 957.

Migne, *Patrologia Graeca [PG]*, Vol. XXXIII, Col. 681.

Motovilov, N.A., *A Conversation of St. Seraphim.* St Nectarios Press, Seattle, 1973 (reprint).

New Catholic Encyclopedia, page 397, Vol. XIV.

Orthodox Christian Catechism (Sofia, 1930), pp. 210-211 [in Bulgarian].

Orthodox Iconography (Belmont, MA: Institute for Modern Greek and Byzantine Studies, 1992 [1977]), pp. 30-35.

Orthodox Iconography, by Dr. Constantine Cavarnos. A short book containing a collection of very fine essays.

Orthodox Life, vol. 26, no. 3 (May-June, 1976), pp. 1-5.

Orthodox Tradition, Vol. XII, No. 2, 41-42.

Orthodox Tradition, Vol. XV, No. 4, pp. 3-9.

Ouspensky, Leonid, and Lossky, Vladimir. The Meaning of Icons. Rev. ed. Crestwood, N.Y.: St. Vladimir's Seminary Press, 1982.

Ouspensky, Leonid, *The Theology of Icons,* Crestwood, N.Y., 1978.

Ouspensky, Leonid. Theology of the Icon. Trans. E. Meyendorff. Crestwood, N.Y.: St. Vladimir's Seminary Press, 1978.

Philokalia, Vol 3, p 322, para 103 (Greek ed.).

Potapov, Victor. "The All-Night Vigil: The Evening Sacrifice." *Russian Orthodox Cathedral of St. John the Baptist*, https://stjohndc.org/en.

Potapov, Victor. "The Beatitudes - The Commandments of Blessedness." *Finding the Way to the Heart*, https://findingthewaytotheheart.blogspot.com.

Rogers, Gregory, *Apostolic Succession*. Ben Lomond, CA: Conciliar Press, 1989. 40 pages. Clearly lays out the Biblical and patristic evidence for apostolic succession. Excellent bibliography.

S. Bolshakoff, *The Foreign Missions of the Russian Orthodox Church,* London, 1943.

Saint Seraphim of Sarov, pp 61-62 (Rus. ed.).

Sergieff, Rev. John Iliytch (St. John of Kronstadt), *My Life in Christ* (Jordanville, N.Y.: Holy Trinity Monastery, 1971), Pt. II, p. 151.

Sermons and Addresses of the Metropolitan Philaret, Moscow, 1844, Part II, p. 87. (In Russian.)

Spiritual Culture, Nos. 20-21 (1924), pp. 155, 163.

St. Abba Dorotheus, "Directions on Spiritual Training," *Early Fathers from the Philokalia,* trans. E. Kadloubovsky and G. E. H. Palmer (London: Faber and Faber Ltd., 1963), p. 176.

St. Basil, *Concerning the Holy Spirit*, Ch. 18.

St. Cyril of Jerusalem, "Catechetical Lectures: On Crucifixion and Burial of Christ," A *Library* of *Fathers* of *the holy*

Catholic Church (Oxford: John Henry Parker, 1845), Vol. 34, Lecture XIII: 36, pp. 161-162.

St. John Chrysostom, "Homilies on the Epistles of Paul to the Corinthians," A *Select Library of Nicene and Post-Nicene Fathers of the Christian Church,* ed. Philip Schaff (Grand Rapids, Michigan: Wm. B. Eerdmans Pub. Co., 1969), Vol. XII, p. 265.

St. John of Damascus, Exposition of the Orthodox Faith," A *Select Library* of *Nicene and Post-Nicene Fathers* of *the Christian Church,* ed. Philip Schaff and Henry Wace (Grand Rapids, Michigan: Wm. B. Eerdmans Pub. Co., 1973), Vol. IX, p. 89.

St. John of Damascus, *On The Divine Images.* Trans. David Anderson. Crestwood, N.Y., 1980. P. 72.

St. John of Damascus. On the Divine Images. Trans. D. Anderson. Crestwood, N.Y.: St. Vladimir's Seminary Press, 1980.

St. Theodore the Studite, *On the Holy Icons.* Crestwood, N.Y., 1981. P. 21.

Synod of Constantinople, 1872. v. Mansi, Coll. *concil.,* vol. 45, 417-546. See also the article by M. Zyzykine: 'L'Eglise orthodoxe et la nation,' *Irenikon,* 1936, pp. 265-77.

The Essence of Orthodox Iconography, by Constantine Kalokyris.

The Mystical Theology of the Eastern Church (London: James Clarke & Co., LTD, 1957), pp. 7-22.

The Notes of Priest A. Elchaninov, YMCA Press, Paris, 1962

The Popes and European Revolution, page 75, Owen Chadwick, Clarendon Press, Oxford, 1981.

The Triumph of the Holy See, page 156, Derek Holmes Burns & Oates, London. 1978

The Twenty One Canons of the Regional Council held in Gangra, *The Rudder (Pedalion)* (Chicago: The Orthodox Christian Educational Society, 1957), p. 523.

Theology of the Icon, Leonid Ouspensky.

Troitsky Ilarion, Archbishop and Holy New Martyr, *The Unity of the Church and the World Conference of Christian Communities.* Montreal: Monastery Press, 1975. 72pp. The best overview on the issue of canonical economy, boundaries of the Church, etc. Archbishop Ilarion is incredibly lucid and Patristic.

Ware, Bishop KALLISTOS, *The Orthodox Church.* Crestwood, NY: St. Vladimir's Press, 1994 (1990), Ch. 12 "The Church of God."

Works of St. Isaac the Syrian, 3rd ed., Sermon 8, p 37.

Printed in Great Britain
by Amazon

8fe8b691-0107-4da5-919b-55d86bf8330dR01